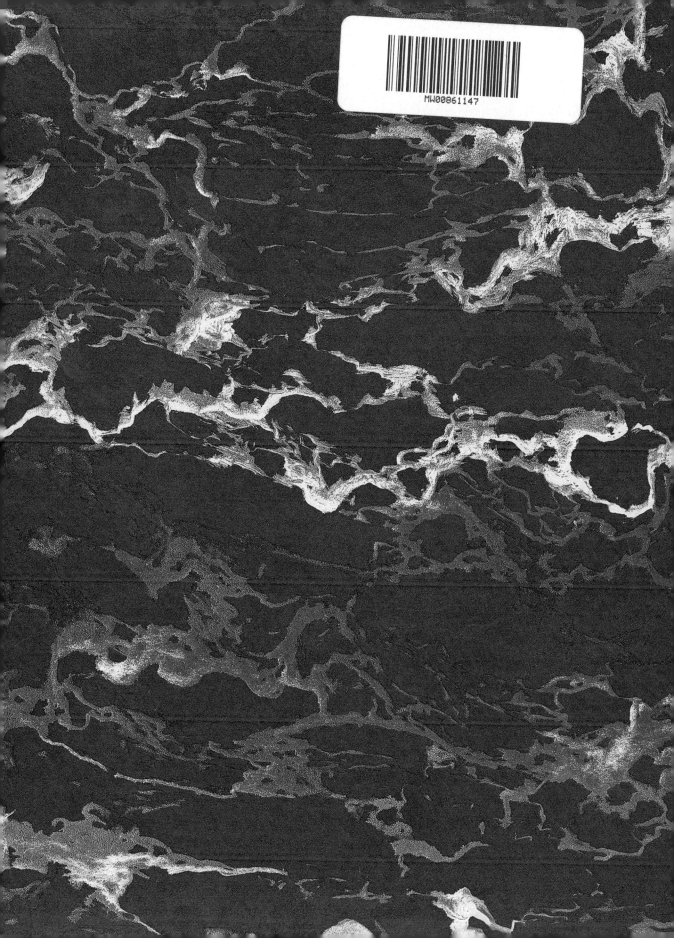

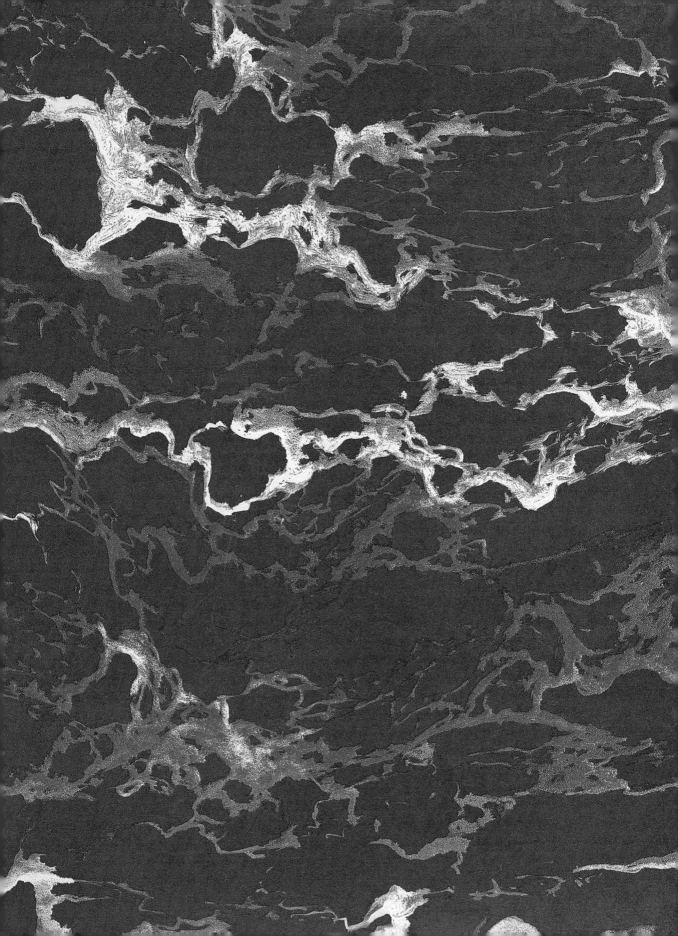

SPATIAL
ALCHEMY

SPATIAL ALCHEMY

Design Your Home to Transform Your Life

OLGA NAIMAN

Artisan | New York

Library of Congress Cataloging-in-Publication Data is on file.

ISBN 978-1-64829-147-0

Design by Giulia Garbin

Artisan books may be purchased in bulk for business, educational, or promotional use. For information, please contact your local bookseller or the Hachette Book Group Special Markets Department at special.markets@hbgusa.com.

The publisher is not responsible for websites (or their content) that are not owned by the publisher.

The Hachette Speakers Bureau provides a wide range of authors for speaking events. To find out more, go to hachettespeakersbureau.com or email HachetteSpeakers@hbgusa.com.

Published by Artisan,
an imprint of Workman Publishing,
a division of Hachette Book Group, Inc.
1290 Avenue of the Americas
New York, NY 10104
artisanbooks.com

The Artisan name and logo are registered trademarks of Hachette Book Group, Inc.

Printed in China on responsibly sourced paper
First printing, March 2025

10 9 8 7 6 5 4 3 2 1

To your Future Self, and to mine

"

We shape
our buildings;
thereafter
they shape us.

"

WINSTON CHURCHILL

Contents

11   Preface: Practical Magic

14   Introduction: My Journey to Spatial Alchemy

18   The Foundations of Spatial Alchemy

38   PART ONE
Energy Matters

66   PART TWO
Dissolving Past Selves

102   PART THREE
Small Moves, Big Shifts

132   PART FOUR
Designing for Emotional Balance

226   PART FIVE
Prioritizing Pleasure

272   Further Reading

274   Acknowledgments

280   Index

286   Photography Credits

Practical Magic

In October 2020, two miraculous things happened to me that were way outside what I was accustomed to manifesting in my life: First, a journalist wrote an article for the *Washington Post* about my work. Then, the article came to the attention of a book publisher, who contacted me to ask if I wanted to write this book.

It seemed like such an anomaly because just four months before, I had felt stuck in many areas of my life, especially my career. I had been working primarily as a stylist, creating compelling spaces for magazine photo shoots and event clients. In recent years it had started to feel like a big piece was missing; I was creating chic spaces, but my soul was left wanting. Deeper questions were percolating inside me, but I didn't know how to marry them with my established styling career. I was trying desperately to shift the stuckness and confusion, to no avail. So I did the only thing that, as an interior designer, I felt a sense of clarity about: I reupholstered five pieces of furniture in my living room. At the time, I had no idea this choice would significantly change the course of my career, and my life. Now, in retrospect, I understand why.

When I decided to redo the furniture, I was in full-on scarcity mindset. My partner, Mike, and I were living off our savings, our work having gone poof in the pandemic. With twins in Zoom kindergarten classes, the upholstery, already in not such great shape, was soon destroyed. Those sofas were hurting my heart—and messing with my self-worth—every time I looked at them. I longed for more beauty in my home.

But I kept hearing my Ukrainian immigrant father's voice: *Don't waste money on stupid stuff. Who cares about the furniture? Save money for more important things, like food!* This is what my ancestral "inner scarcity" voice sounds like. I was petrified with uncertainty.

But then something else rose up: a voice I have come to think of as my "Future Self" voice. It came from a woman inside me who had moved through my current crisis and was now living in the home of her dreams, with a career that connected her design work with her soul. I might not have had faith in myself in that moment, but I somehow had faith in her. So I took a deep breath and just did it.

A string of fortuitous coincidences occurred soon after I made this move, including the article and invitation to write the book you are holding in your hands. What floored me the most was how it all just came to me. It felt as if I had stepped into a new reality that was very different from the one I'd felt trapped inside.

I began to wonder if, perhaps, the furniture had something to do with it—if there was a correlation between the emotional shifts that the reupholstery made possible and the events that were unfolding.

On a surface level, you could say I was simply reupholstering pieces of furniture. People reupholster furniture all the time. So what? Yet, on a wider, creational level, the choice was an unconscious declaration to the universe: "I am READY."

I was as surprised as anyone that this Future Self thing actually worked. Could there really be a cause-and-effect relationship between the design choices I was making for my home and the doors opening in my life? Asking this question is what turned me from a stylist and interior designer into a Spatial Alchemist.

An insatiable curiosity to test out exactly how this approach worked kicked in. I made more moves in my house, both big and small, that were designed to disrupt unwanted psychological patterns. I was tracking how these moves affected both my sense of self-worth and my ability to meet my emotional needs, and how that carried over into other parts of my life. Working in concert with my home allowed my life to expand and deepen more within the next three years than in the previous two decades spent engaging in a wide range of healing modalities. I was beginning to understand that my home was the missing link. By previously designing my home based on style and function alone, I hadn't been tapping into its full potential.

This realization was the birth of Spatial Alchemy. As I began integrating these principles more and more with design clients and through online teaching, I noticed a commonality: Unexpected doors began to open in people's lives that they would trace back to the shifts they were making in their home. They had tapped into the alchemical power of their environment, working on the level of energy in addition to the level of aesthetics, and magical things were happening in their lives.

When you design your home to align with your deepest intention for yourself, you are deciding to call this intention forth. Like me, you are telling the universe, "I am READY."

When your home is aligned with your desired future, you step into that reality with more ease. I styled this tableau with symbols meant to intentionally magnetize more abundance.

My Journey to Spatial Alchemy

Alchemy predates science. In the medieval period, among other pursuits, alchemists experimented with turning base metals such as lead into far more precious, highly sought-after materials, namely gold and silver. The practice was not, as you might think, born strictly out of greed or a lust for wealth. On the contrary, alchemy was a quest toward spiritual enlightenment and rebirth, with the lead and the gold as stand-ins for the self. You are the lead. You are also the gold. To paraphrase Paracelsus, a sixteenth-century Swiss-German physician and alchemist, you only transmute *without* what you have first transmuted *within*.

In my heart, I am an alchemist. Like the medieval practitioners of alchemy, I believe in the upleveling of everyday materials into substances of higher value. When I realized that it was possible to turn metaphorical lead into gold, I found my burning passion. Since then, it has been how I approach everything I do in my professional life, and in my home, too.

It works like this: Take one rather familiar thing, unlock its composition, and then experiment with the essential ingredients and proportions, adjusting them until the once ordinary thing is transformed into something extraordinary. This new substance is infused with new meaning and greater worth and emits a higher energy and more magnetic appeal than the substance you started with. In the context of my Spatial Alchemy practice, the

material is you—and the laboratory for conducting its transformation is your home.

In one way or another, I've been practicing Spatial Alchemy my whole life. As the daughter of psychiatrists—my father was a cognitive behavioral therapist and my mother a psychodynamic therapist—I grew up steeped in the language of brain health. Psychology was the everyday mode of conversation in our house, where we regularly discussed emotional awareness.

Yet my childhood was spent in a constant state of flux. After my family came to the United States as refugees from the Soviet Union in 1977, we moved around every two years. While my parents were settling in and stepping into their American dream, I never managed to feel fully settled. As I'll go into in more depth in the pages that follow, I eventually learned to turn this core wound into gold. How? Through the power of my home. I came to recognize how I could design my surroundings not only to emotionally regulate myself but also to expand what's possible in my life. We will explore that process in full later in this book, but for now, a bit of background.

From a young age, I found myself drawn to the world of interior design. In the fifth grade, I discovered the home decor section at the local library. Every day after school, I would pore over books filled with photographs of grand residences all over the world. When I turned fifteen, my parents gave me a budget to redecorate my bedroom, and I proceeded to refresh the whole house.

Though I went on to study clinical psychology at university, my love for interior design held sway, leading me to a job as an assistant in the decorating department at *House Beautiful* upon graduation. My design work landed on the cover when I was just twenty-five, a major coup at a time (the late 1990s) when magazines were still the primary arbiters of style.

But craving a level of depth that magazines were not providing, after a few years I moved to London to pursue a master's degree in scenography (essentially, installation art and set design) at Central Saint Martins. Studying theater helped me put the human element at the center of my ideas and design from there. It trained me to visually narrate how characters and spaces change over time. For the next two decades, I brought my design and theater backgrounds to bear for commercial and editorial clients. As a freelance interior stylist, I designed compelling interiors within the context of whatever brief was thrown at me, creating any style the client asked for.

In my personal life I was involved in various forms of traditional therapy (psychotherapy, cognitive behavioral therapy, and Jungian therapy among them) and studied many different disciplines, incorporating science (quantum physics, brain chemistry, neuroaesthetics, clinical psychology, and more) in equal measure

with spiritual practices (shamanic rituals, Tantra, Kabbalah, and others). I wanted to explore the edges of consciousness and get to the heart of how personal transformation is accelerated. What I found was that when you combine the paths of science (logic) and spirituality (heart-wisdom) with the objective of transforming your life, you begin to expand more rapidly than with either study alone.

As I brought these teachings and discoveries to bear on my own life, Spatial Alchemy was in its research and development phase, largely a response to a few big questions: How can I take my findings from all the disciplines and theories I've been studying and put them into practice? Can I translate the insights gained from therapy and other healing modalities into my physical environment— aka my home—to uplevel my life? And can I do this for interior design clients, too? The answer, I was thrilled to discover, is a resounding *yes*.

In the pages that follow, I'll show you how your aha moment in therapy can crystallize in the layout of your living room. That your subconscious communicates through the art on your walls. That it's possible to gain traction in your career by rearranging your home office. I believe that if we can transmute the ordinary into the extraordinary through the process of refinement, as the ancient alchemists did, we can better not only our homes but ultimately ourselves.

When I decided to reupholster several torn and frayed pieces of furniture in my former living room, even though it felt extravagant, everything started to shift for the better in my life. For me, this crystallized the connection between the home and the psyche, and led to the birth of *Spatial Alchemy*.

THE FOUNDATIONS OF SPATIAL ALCHEMY

At the core of my approach to interior design is one radically simple idea: Your home is a tool for personal transformation and positive change. By tapping into its full potential, you may in turn harness your own. I see the home as a portal between our inner world and the big, crazy, uncontrollable world beyond it. Home is the one place that you can actively and immediately shape.

In consultations with both friends and clients, I began to understand why most people struggle with interior design: They look outward to the space first, rather than inward. With Spatial Alchemy, instead of focusing only on the function and aesthetics of a space, I aim to help people deepen their awareness of who they are becoming. We see how we can refine and reposition what they already own, to meet their current needs and desires more easily. In this way, you can move from wanting something in the future to creating a sense of already having it. When you cultivate a relationship with the energy you want to embody, through your home, you start to see more of it coming into your life, in profound and often unexpected ways.

Designing our homes with the intention of stepping into the most fulfilled version of ourselves allows us to address our needs and desires all at once, on all levels—spiritual, emotional, mental, and physical. The true power of home design lies in recognizing—and seizing—the opportunity to build the life you want, starting from the interior and working your way outward. As within, so without.

You may be wondering whether the way you design your most intimate spaces can really affect the way you move through the world. Without a doubt, it can make your life more fulfilling, efficient, rewarding, and productive, shifting you out of "stuckness" and stagnancy. Using your home as a dynamic, interactive tool keeps the opportunities for growth flowing.

In applying the basic principles of Spatial Alchemy to your living space, you are creating a system that tips your inner scale. Self-worth is the "gold" that alchemists speak of. It's the precious substance that leads you to the next level of intuitive awareness, which allows you to play the game of life with joy and skill. And it all starts with examining the essential elements that make up *you*.

The Process

Throughout this book, you'll be taken through the steps that I use with my clients to transform their lives by strategically shifting their homes. It is written and designed as a linear progression that builds on itself as you undertake each step. The effects will compound once you begin recognizing how upgrades in your home kick-start a domino effect in other aspects of your life.

This process unfolds in several stages and begins with a set of questions to help you clarify your intentions for your life. The point is to conjure your Future Self—a term you'll see used frequently in this book. You'll then take this Future Self energy and learn to plug it into your home. Here's how it's done:

Tapping into the Future Self starts with articulating your desires. To create clear and concise intentions for yourself, first identify where your home is supporting that Future Self energy and where it is sapping it.

The next step is to disrupt your old patterns. Take note of any outdated identities and mindset patterns that reinforce your personal status quo, then dissolve them by removing items from your home that represent those identities. This often takes more than one round; keep in mind that it's a progression, not a one-time upgrade.

Once you've cleared your home of things that are no longer serving you, it's time to seed your new patterns. To consciously design your spaces for the emerging Future Self identity you want to bring into being, introduce a few new items that will help embed those new patterns and start to generate momentum.

Next, you'll address how to meet your emotional needs by putting together a home that responds to what you long to experience more of in your life. The goal is to build an emotionally secure base from which to grow and expand.

Finally, after going through all the steps of dissolving old patterns and solidifying new ones (known as *solve et coagula*, which you'll learn more about starting on page 68), you can claim your pleasure by way of the home. Pulling it all together in a way that turns you on and brings you the most delightful, feel-good energy is a key to accelerating your transformation.

1.
ARTICULATE
YOUR DESIRES

2.
DISRUPT YOUR
OLD PATTERNS

3.
SEED YOUR
NEW PATTERNS

4.
MEET YOUR
EMOTIONAL NEEDS

5.
CLAIM YOUR
PLEASURE

Life Science 101

Your home is your laboratory, and you are the life scientist. You are looking for a cause-and-effect relationship, assessing the correlation between what you are doing in your home and what is shifting in your life. Throughout this book, I'll be encouraging you to center your focus on your Future Self as you approach the design of your home. I see your Future Self as a state of being as much as a state of having. It is the state that you feel viscerally in your body when your intention for yourself becomes a reality. I will ask you to engage in exercises along the way, each geared to give you actionable advice and takeaways you can apply to your home as you engage in the process of Spatial Alchemy. For now, however, let's begin with a moment of self-reflection, to help bring clarity to the effect your home has on both your body and your psyche.

Imagine for a moment what happens when you neglect your home. You may find yourself living with things that literally get in your way, holding on to chipped or broken items that you put off replacing, unconsciously settling for less than what you *truly* want to live with. It's easy to see how this scenario would fail to motivate or excite you.

Now reverse that vision. Picture what it would be like to proactively set up your house guided only by how you want to feel.

Let's say your life is feeling very chaotic and you are looking for more support. As a proactive measure, give yourself what you want to receive. Rather than simmer in a state of perpetual longing, begin to design, step by step, the feeling of "I'm already supported" into your home. What does that feeling look like when anchored into form? What styling choices would you make to make your home feel more supportive? As a first, very small step, you might incorporate balanced, symmetrical pairs of items in focal points throughout your home—bedside lamps, for example, or candlesticks on the mantel. You are learning to program your environment to achieve a specific outcome. Soon, more balance begins to come into your experience. Life starts to feel more ordered, in both expected and unexpected ways.

In my experience, it is faster to make changes in my physical surroundings than it is to change myself. If I am shifting my home with specific *big-picture* intention, it will have more of an effect on my life than if I design for style alone. When you focus on making your home resonate with who you are becoming, you begin to see it in a different way. It goes from an inanimate collection of objects to a deeper extension of you, a living being whose essence reflects your personal narrative as well as your future.

Some of this may sound a little heady, even trippy, if you are not familiar with energetics or have never worked with them, but bear with me. Even among the biggest skeptics, the process starts to make sense once you begin playing around with it.

It's important to note that you don't have to buy anything new in this process. Instead, you can use what you already have in a more conscious way, adjusting and calibrating. Once you begin to feel the results of these shifts, you start to generate momentum toward more of the things (in this case, feelings) that you want.

How will you know you're on the right track? When you notice yourself feeling more alive and attuned to more pleasure in your home. Next come more recurring signs, symbols, and coincidences. Each of these is a marker of the universe speaking back to you, in response to your raised awareness. You are strengthening your understanding of the way that "matter" (the stuff that surrounds you within your home) affects energy (the way you feel inside), and how this has *everything* to do with how you present yourself to the world at large. In essence, this is what the ancient alchemists called transmutation—and what I call modern-day magic at work.

This chair's fuzzy texture soothes my nervous system, and the upholstered arms invite nestling. Sitting here, with my feet on the ottoman, I feel as if I'm being held. The chair's sculptural shape keeps it from feeling overstuffed and dominating the room.

Your Home Has Your Back

Your relationship with your home is primal, fundamental, and foundational to your whole being, naturally forming the template you carry throughout your life. Before you can bring your Future Self into being, however, you'll need to look to your past.

No matter our background, most of us begin adulthood by caring for ourselves the way we were cared for as children. Our childhood experiences influence how we establish our adult homes, and how much care we attach to them. How were you cared for? If your childhood longings were not met at home, know that teaching yourself to flip the script and fulfill them for your adult self is possible—and invaluable. The key comes in awareness.

Many of us are not aware of the emotional baggage we carry from our earliest days. We may have unresolved feelings, fears, or self-doubt perpetuated by the harsh voice of the inner critic. Over time, feelings of unworthiness can affect our emotional growth and development, manifesting in unwanted patterns, lack of motivation, confusion, and stagnation.

When we teach our adult selves to feel and regulate our emotions, we exist in a space of conscious response rather than being hemmed in by unconscious reactivity. We develop agency over our responses, meeting challenges with an open heart, having confidence in our decisions, and feeling secure in our ability to develop healthy and meaningful relationships.

It took me forty-five years to allow myself to experience a deep sense of intimacy with my home. Growing up, I longed to be held, and I yearned for tenderness. I was raised by busy parents hustling to make a living. Our Soviet immigrant family moved constantly. No matter which home we were in, the space itself never felt stable or particularly emotionally supportive. I never sensed that my home had my back. In adulthood, I gradually learned to develop a relationship with my home built on a solid foundation of emotional well-being—where I now have the capacity to feel secure, nurtured, inspired, and restored, the way that any good parent would make their child feel. This is how I've come to know that re-parenting can impact every aspect of life. When we begin to consciously design our homes, we consciously shape ourselves, regardless of our past.

As a first step in my re-parenting process, I tried to imagine what it might feel like for my house to give me a hug. What would that look like? In response, I placed a chair near the front door, in a spot where I can sit as soon as I enter, so I'm not hopping on one leg taking off my shoes. This telegraphs an immediate welcome and attention to my needs. I brought in what I've termed an "emotional regulation chair" in the living room, where I retreat when I feel distraught or emotionally drained. I placed baskets of fuzzy blankets and throws nearby, to hold me when I feel less than whole. In the bedroom, I swapped out old bed linens for new ones that feel great on my skin. The cumulative effect of these changes? An abundance of TLC has been programmed in my home and is working its way through every room. This is practical, tangible re-parenting.

Since then, my home has been emotionally supporting me in ways that I never could have imagined as a child. When you give yourself what you long for, you weave the process of meeting those primal needs into your system, strand by strand. You also begin to receive them from other sources, fostering an environment that supports both your growth and your social-emotional health. Programming this level of emotional well-being into your home lets you reap its benefits beyond its confines as well.

Re-parenting isn't about blaming your parents, which only gets you so far. Rather, it's a tool to access more personal empowerment and a form of intentional patterning. I believe the home is the microcosm of every single pattern you see in your life. You can't fully love, honor, and value yourself if your home is full of design decisions that run you down. The re-parenting process helps us exit the loop of treating ourselves the way we were treated as children and respond instead from expanded awareness. If we grew up in a home where we felt nurtured and encouraged, we can also learn to mirror and integrate those patterns into our present-day experience, as another way

of extending the emotional regulation. The more responsibility you take to parent your inner child, the more you are activating your solid inner parent.

Can you take time to explore where you came from and the impact your earliest environment may have had on present-day you? You may think, *I had a loving childhood—nothing to see there*, but nevertheless, certain effects remain in place, however subtle. Likewise, examine how you experienced comfort at home. As children, we take in all kinds of messages. Think about how your childhood home(s) impacted your body and mind at that time, and how that may have carried over as you crossed into adulthood.

- What was your childhood home like? Can you describe it in a few words?

- Did you like being at home as a child? Were you happy when you came home from school and walked through the door?

- Did you feel safe and secure at home?

- Was your childhood home beautiful to you?

Now, consider how your answers to the questions above are reflected in your current home. What are the similarities and differences between your current and childhood homes?

Take some time to examine and contemplate your answers. This is how you can learn to be a better caretaker to yourself going forward, even more loving, steady, and dependable.

To welcome more softness into your life, consider your home's corners, which are often overlooked as places to retreat to and reset. This upholstered daybed in my current living room invites tender loving self-care with sink-into-me pillows and a mohair throw.

Building a Secure Base

Attachment theory goes beyond parenting to incorporate the ways in which we learn to connect with all humans. Each of us is primed from birth to do so. Naturally, this primal need initially manifests in our relationships with our parents and earliest caregivers. When we experience secure attachment throughout infancy and our childhood years, we learn to create a solid base, and in turn, to feel stable, safe, self-confident, and truly loved. (You may have heard of examples of early attachment parenting including baby wearing, co-sleeping, and on-demand feeding.)

Psychotherapist and author Jessica Fern, an expert on attachment theory, describes secure attachment as the embodied experience of a grounded, centered base from which we form lasting relationships with others. Attachment is also critical in developing our self-esteem; the two exist in a positive feedback loop, in fact, a cycle that facilitates emotional balance and growth.

Not everyone experiences secure attachment in childhood, however. According to Fern, "When we have experienced attachment insecurity with caregivers, our primary relationship with our self can become severed. . . . Attachment ruptures and trauma can also leave lasting marks on our psyches,

distorting our sense of self through the beliefs that we do not matter, that we are flawed, broken, unworthy, or too much while, simultaneously, not enough."

Fern believes that our ability to form relationships is influenced by the physical homes we grew up in. The way you consistently felt within your childhood home—whether you were plagued with residual stress or tension or were able to rest and relax comfortably within it—correlates with the way your nervous system developed. Think back to your experience of your home as a child, whether or not you felt safe and secure within the physical space, how it sounded, how it smelled, how crowded or empty it was, who lived with you within it, what your relationships were like, what rituals and customs you practiced. Each of these factors contribute to the sense of attachment you experience in adulthood, both to your current home and to people in your life.

Many people must consciously rebuild and repair their attachment styles as adults in order to establish personal relationships with more ease. Fortunately, it's possible to teach oneself secure attachment as an adult. Once I realized that I could use my home as a tool to walk myself out of emotionally debilitating relationship patterns, I went all in. After years of repeating the same emotional patterns with different partners, I needed to create an internal center for myself, rather than looking for grounding from an external source. I realized I could style my home to mirror the secure attachment I wanted to embody. I wanted to know what security and self-worth viscerally felt like, so I set up my home as the secure base I had longed for as a child. Re-balancing became my game plan. If I could show up with a greater level of love for myself, I thought, maybe my relationships could become less fraught, more joyful. Perhaps I might even give myself what I was longing to receive from my partner first, and then see how this might affect our relationship.

I walked through my home, noting every spot where I was obviously neglecting myself on some level. I wrote up a lengthy (initially overwhelming) list. Slowly, I worked my way through it, tackling the easy stuff first. I tidied up my messy nightstand drawer, and replaced lightbulbs that were too dim. I observed how my body responded to each small move, celebrating its positive responses. I went on to more involved adjustments: shifting my living room furniture to focus more on the view outside than on the TV, buying myself an emotional regulation chair (see page 25), choosing a solid dresser for the bedroom,

and adding a pair of oversize, stately footed vases to program a bold and self-assured energy into the home office. After each upgrade, I would pause to register how my body and my heart felt. My relationship with myself grew deeper and more intimate when I had a home that supported me when I felt destabilized.

When you feel like your home has your back, your relationships with others become easier, and you consistently bulk up the self-regulation muscle. By programming your surroundings to address your emotional needs, you are reinforcing—or in some cases, developing from the ground up—the secure base muscle, strengthening your emotional core, and upleveling your self-worth. I invite you to sit with the following questions:

- What's around you that's causing you to feel destabilized?

- What in your home feels neglected? What have you been ignoring? How does this correlate with the ways in which you neglect and ignore yourself?

- Where do you feel a lack of embodied connection with your home? What can you do to feel more intimacy with your home?

An Introduction to the Four Realms

This book is rooted in the ancient transformational practice of alchemy, which itself is strongly linked to the Kabbalah. As such, the structure of the Spatial Alchemy process is mapped onto the Kabbalah's concept of the four realms: physical, mental, emotional, and spiritual. In my years of studying creational principles across many traditions, the key takeaway has been that the fundamentals are universal. I have gathered what I've learned about the spiritual, emotional, and mental realms and transposed it into practical, everyday life by way of the physical realm.

- The physical realm refers to matter you can see, touch, and affect, which includes your body, and is the most consistent and tangible of the four realms. It is the manifest world that we see around us.

- The mental realm represents pure thought. It is the sum of your opinions, goals, values, judgments, and beliefs, which combine to create your identity.

- The emotional realm is the wide, wide world of feelings, which color our perceptions of reality.

- The spiritual realm is the least understood, because it is at once every thing and no thing. It encompasses the unmanifest world of nightly dreams, your subconscious mind, your sense of your soul, all energy, your relationship with a higher power, your intuition, and beyond.

The human "you" is a combination of all four realms: a spiritual being simultaneously having a physical, mental, and emotional experience. We navigate these realms simultaneously and daily, often without realizing it. Once you train yourself to recognize the individual realms, you can sharpen your understanding of how they work in tandem. And the more you create resonance between your physical, mental, emotional, and spiritual realms, the more easily your visions will come to fruition.

Spatial Alchemy teaches you how to navigate and harness the realms to create a home that resonates not only with your aesthetic sensibilities and functional requirements but also with your deeper dreams and desires. A home that feels not only good but also magnetic.

SPIRITUAL

MENTAL

YOU

EMOTIONAL

PHYSICAL

THE THREE QUESTIONS

The following self-assessment exercise forms the backbone of the Spatial Alchemy process and is designed to teach you to merge identities with the Future Self. It goes beyond material choices, digging deep to discover what lies beneath them.

Keep in mind that it takes courage to state your intentions, to clearly and honestly express what you wish to change in your life. The reward is even more of the inner wisdom you need to move forward toward the version of you who feels fulfilled and supported by life, who feels even more *whole*, aka your Future Self.

I developed these three questions to help you see how your home is—or is not—reflecting the vision of your Future Self. The more life experiences I am longing for or frustrated at not being able to create for myself, the more rounds of these questions I go through. They shift the focus from me to my home.

QUESTION 1
What do you long to experience more of in your life?

Generally, answers to this question fall into three categories: optimized health, wealth, or relationships. You want to pick one of these categories to focus on for this exercise, rather than grouping them all together. Keep your statements concise, and err on the side of simplicity (for example, "I want to find a life partner," or "I want to pivot to a new career").

QUESTION 2
Why do you think you don't yet have what you want?

Sit with your thoughts for a while on this one and lean in to the intentions you just expressed before directing your attention inward. The objective is to identify personal traits and habits that may be self-limiting, whether conscious or not. Use your intuition to tap into your inner truths and unpack whatever is standing in the way of change. Listing your obstacles allows you to acknowledge them more directly than when they're floating around in your head. Now distill all the reasons into three sentences that get to the essence of what is stopping you from having what you want. This insight helps you develop an accurate understanding of yourself and a recognition of what you perceive as impediments.

QUESTION 3

How are those patterns materializing inside your home?

Shift your focus to your own feeling of stuckness. Close your eyes. As you reopen them, slowly take in everything in the room around you, zeroing in on troublesome or neglected spots. Identify and take note of things in your home that feel out of alignment with you. Where is your home reinforcing your stuckness more than your vision? (If it's not apparent quite yet, don't worry. The following section goes into depth about how you can begin to see your home from an objective point of view.

An example of how this works: After answering the first question, my client Tamara expressed that she wanted to move forward in her career but was feeling stuck, as she was repeatedly passed over for promotions. She struggled to answer the second question, but it was clear her managers didn't believe she was ready for a more senior position. When she reached the third question, she realized that she was surrounded by items that weren't expressing who she is. Her wife had strong design opinions, and because she didn't, Tamara felt it was easier to hang back and avoid arguing. She hadn't made the connection that taking more of an active role in her home and its furnishings might help her invite more leadership at work as well. To be taken seriously at work, she'd have to start taking herself more seriously at home. Once we concluded the exercise, Tamara replaced some key items with choices that were more aligned with the senior executive role she wanted to embody. By planting the seeds at home for her career growth, she took the steps to promote her *self* first.

WHAT TO DO WHEN THE ANSWERS
DON'T COME EASILY

▲ ▲ ▲

All of us fall into "I don't know" responses and freeze there. The way to get out of that sticky place is to begin by acknowledging what you *do* know. Think of just one thing that you knew for sure when you read the three questions on the previous pages. It may be a small, seemingly insignificant truth. Stay with that one answer and explore it. By accepting and honoring this truth, you encourage more responses to follow.

If, however, your responses to these questions failed to bring about a lightning bolt of clarity and intuition, don't sweat it. Avoid judging yourself. This book is geared toward helping you identify your needs and learn how to address and fulfill them without shame or embarrassment. Take your time and move slowly through the process. As an innate alchemist, remember that the way to hone your intuition is to cultivate a space of receptivity. Stay curious, patient, and engaged. Don't push for answers if they aren't coming. Once the inner self feels safe, the answers should reveal themselves, and increasingly, you will be able to access your inherent wisdom.

Much like the way interior designers use strong colors as focal points to draw the eye forward, as you make your way through the pages of this book, remember to keep your eye on where you're headed—the Future Self—and embrace the steady progression it will take to get there.

Making Room for Love

When I look back on my previous bedrooms through the eyes of an alchemist, I clearly see how my design choices were affecting my life, positively and negatively. Pictured here are bedrooms in the homes where I've lived over the last two decades, from a rental apartment when I was a single city girl to an apartment that became a home for four when my partner and twins entered the picture, to a longer-than-intended rental home in the country. They were all featured in national magazines and considered chic, but in reality, these rooms were anything but magnetic. Take the edgy boudoir in figure 1, opposite, as an example. I realize now how some of the elements I chose were hindering, not helping, my desire for lasting love and partnership.

Fig. 1 No Man's Land

In the Brooklyn apartment where I lived in my twenties, I was designing to please no one but myself. It appears as if I'm perfectly content all alone in this reclusive-looking bedroom, nestled among my soft-colored linens and mismatched lamps. And those stacked cinder blocks holding up the bed, doing double duty as visible shoe storage? The message was clear: I was not interested in settling down and settling in; in fact, I could pick up and leave at a moment's notice, pumps in hand. To arrange this space with a partner in mind, I would have replaced my kooky lamps with a matching set on either side of the bed, to represent the kind of calm, solid energy I craved. A bedframe with a headboard would have allowed my body to lean back, feel held in place, and anchor into my life.

Fig. 2 Together but Alone

A decade later, I had found a mate and started a family in our city apartment. The matching bedside tables were more stabilizing, and the color palette stronger and more active. Yet I still felt alone in this bedroom (and often, in our partnership). The artwork is a clue to my state of mind: the piece over the bed features the head of a man having his tooth removed while being held down, and along the side of the bed is a series of framed butterflies pinned in place. Clearly, I felt hemmed in. The matching tables lacked drawers; we either had to let things pile up or get out of bed to find what we needed. Chaos set in, and friction built up between us. My partner, Mike, and I felt unsupported and restless—exactly the opposite of how we should've felt in the bedroom. Again, without knowing it, I had one foot on the gas pedal and the other on the brake.

Fig. 3 Starting to See the Connection

This bedroom represents a turning point, as I began to understand how I could use interior design to magnetize the life I long for. After Mike and I made it through a rough patch, we decided to design our bed together. A velvet bedframe delivered the lushness we both needed; orange also references the second chakra, a creational portal that supports intimacy (more on the chakra system on page 140). To ground us and soften any end-of-day edges, we positioned the bed close to the floor, laid the pillows flat, and kept the linens simple. (Mike pulled me back from my tendency toward pattern.) I added striped artwork in activating colors to keep the room—and our partnership—from feeling dull. Together, these adjustments represent the integration of desire and design.

Fig. 1

Fig. 2

Fig. 3

PART ONE

ENERGY MATTERS

Your home is a direct reflection of your psyche. Shift your home, and you shift your psyche.

Spatial Alchemy is designed to help you positively affect the psyche of the alchemist (you) with awareness and precision. But first, you need to learn how to perceive and actively engage with energy.

Like me, you've probably been trained to approach life through your logical mind, but anyone can learn to expand their energetic proficiency. The first step to working with energy is simply acknowledging that it exists, even though you can't see or touch it. Energy is something we all sense, though it's a lot easier to sense other people's energy than our own.

While many people dismiss energetic awareness as airy-fairy woo-woo, I consider it a highly practical and time-efficient art. Tuning in to the energies around you is an essential step in learning how to use your home to its fullest potential: as a vehicle for self-actualization. Realizing this was a pivot point in my life. For years, my approach to life was largely mental, informed by my early grounding in science and psychology. Yet that approach fell flat once I began to understand the way energy works with the physical world. That's when things really started to shift.

With practice, I could perceive the energetic signature of every item in my home by how each made me feel. I realized that every design choice I made was moving me either toward what I wanted to feel or away from it. As I began removing anything in my home that contributed to my stuckness and creating more space for myself, I became aware that my home was helping me move in the direction of my desired outcomes. The alignment of the four realms left me feeling energized, and not only in the physical sense. Things felt less random, more clear. There was also a sense of heightened beauty and more emotional support, which fed my determination and resolve.

Once you can recognize the energy around you, you are ready to mold it using your home. You will begin to identify physical things as expressions of specific energy. Clutter, for example, is the embodiment of stagnant or calcified energy.

Remember, you are the programmer of your own life, and your home is the program you have the most control over (much more than you have over your partner, your children, your boss, or your body, for that matter). You don't see the program, but it is there, reflecting your beliefs about your self-worth, your thoughts, and your limitations. Once you become aware of the program, you can adjust it to positively impact your entire life. When you are proficient at recognizing energy, you begin to see with your own "knowing," which goes beyond observing with your eyes to enlarging your field of awareness. Keep in mind that there is no right or wrong in the realm of the spirit; acknowledging that, engaging your curiosity, and releasing any effort to "get it right" has a profound effect.

On the following pages, you will learn:

- How to tune in to energetic channels and identify where your home is feeding (or sapping) your energy

- How to program the energy of the Future Self into your home

- How to use deliberate design to make your home feel aligned with your soul

- The difference between embodied creation and manifestation

Can You Feel It?

Energy works on all levels—conscious, subconscious, and primal—but it is not something you process in your logical brain. Our bodies *feel* the energy of spaces through the heart, the gut, the pores, and the mind, whether we acknowledge it or not. This is why energy is so difficult to put into words. It is more connected to our sensing and feeling right brain than to our language- and logic-focused left brain.

We are all born energetic beings. The human body is designed to be both an antenna for sensing energy and a barometer for measuring and forecasting it. The more attention you pay to this feature of your technology, the more you begin to decode its various settings. And the more aware you are of energy, the more efficient you are with a very precious resource: time.

It helps to distinguish between body-sustaining energy, which we get from food and oxygen, and soul-sustaining energy, which is the sustenance of creation. You can survive without it, but you will not thrive. Thriving comes with a sense of being in sync. Your body knows this feeling: Think back to the last time you felt it, a definitive inner *yes*. Clock this "in sync" feeling, which will guide you in your interior design choices as you move through this book.

Your home is the safest place in the world for you to practice discerning and then harnessing soul-sustaining energy. Think of receiving a gift that clearly shows the gift-giver chose it just for you. Those qualities—of intention, attention, and care—are potent forms of energy, and so it's no surprise that a thoughtful present uplifts your soul. When most people say a home has "good energy," this is what they mean. You walk in and immediately sense the abundance of intention, attention, and care that the space has been infused with. It feels good. You want to stay.

Your home is either feeding your energy or taking energy away from you. When you are being fed, you feel nurtured and sustained. When you are not being fed, you feel frustrated, confused, and unsettled. Ideally, you will develop a relationship with your home where it is feeding you and you are feeding it. This is the positive energy feedback loop of a healthy environment.

TUNE IN TO THE CHANNEL

If you think that you can't sense energy, think again. You can—you're probably just not aware of it. The visualization below is designed to teach you to see how your body responds to specific prompts. Understanding your subtle responses helps you make more aligned choices in your home, and brings you out of the design confusion that many of us get stuck in.

1. Close your eyes and imagine your own home when it's at its very best. Nothing is broken or awaiting repair, pathways are clear and unobstructed, things work optimally, clutter is minimal, natural light is streaming through the windows, the air feels fresh. It's not a rigid or sterile environment but rather one that's comfortable and easy to be in. Good energy flows. The home feels "lived in" (in the best sense of the phrase). The space has been loved and cared for like a living being.

Notice the sensations that came up in your body. Deeper breathing? Goose bumps? Tingling? All are the hallmarks of your personal creation-mode signal. Remember this feeling. This is what it feels like to tune in to the "positive" (inner *yes*) energetic channel of your space.

2. Now imagine your home at its worst. What you feel when you look around it is a crushing sense of overwhelm. There are so many things demanding your attention, you don't know where to turn. You feel like you don't have the time, money, space, or energy to remedy the situation, if you even knew where to begin. In response, you shut down, get stuck in the "Why bother?" cycle, which often extends into other parts of your life. Nothing changes. This is one of the markers of survival mode. Clock your bodily responses.

3. Go back and forth between the two sensation channels described above to note their differences. You are becoming aware of energy through the realm of intuition and awareness. This felt sense is a kind of inner knowing that exists beyond verbal expression, a form of nonverbal communication that is central to the spiritual realm.

The central point of
energy in this room is the
image of the portal—a
classic and potent symbol
of transformation. The
two large pieces of art on
either side of the focal
image were chosen to
accentuate its colors, as
was the long yellow pillow
on the sofa. Together,
they form an invisible
triangle that surrounds
the portal and amplifies its
symbolic message. Even
the lamps are energizing,
particularly the wavy lines
within them. I designed
a loose slipcover for the
substantial sofa to bring
softness into the clean-
lined space.

Feng Shui & Spatial Alchemy

Throughout history, many cultures have created systems of bringing space and energy together to produce specific results. Perhaps one of the most prominent among them is feng shui, with roots in Taoism, an ancient Chinese philosophy. There are dozens of approaches that fit within the practice, but they all share the same fundamental concepts, primarily the focus on auspicious chi, or life-force energy, in our surroundings. Feng shui masters and ancient temple builders understood how to use light, placement, flow, color, material, and sacred geometry to touch the deeper chords of the human soul. "Feng shui believes that home affects life and mind and body," says Anjie Cho, a feng shui practitioner and author of *Mindful Homes*. As she explains, when you place things in specific positions in your home, manifestation leans in your direction.

Many of the concepts central to feng shui are practical. This is what makes them so genius, in my view. We all know good spatial energy when we feel it: When you walk into a space whose designer understands not only how the subtlety of color works but also how the body moves in the space, you sense the deliberate use of energy.

Feng shui practitioner and author Amanda Gibby Peters of Simple Shui considers the home a great untapped resource. When anything in your life needs to shift, Gibby Peters says, simple adjustments in your home can help it do so. "Once you start to treat your home as another member of the family," she says, "life improves, inside and out." Having studied several approaches to feng shui, Gibby Peters believes that the distinctions between them are less important than the auspicious chi, which grounds them all. "Whatever propels you forward to do something positive in your space, anything that's going to reinforce or enhance whatever you're trying to improve or trigger, it all works," she says. "Feng shui is about putting yourself in favorable circumstances and creating an environment that encourages success. That's all."

So if you were to draw a Venn diagram of feng shui and Spatial Alchemy, where would they intersect? In Spatial Alchemy, the language of energy is fundamental to the conversation you are having with your home, as it is in feng shui. Though there are cultural and aesthetic differences, the foundations of both systems have overlaps—primarily, that each practice considers the way that energy flows into the home and moves within it, and how that movement affects the home's inhabitants. In other words, how the state of our home is tied to our emotional and mental states, which, in turn, is tied to manifestation. Both practices are built on intentionality; when deliberate adjustments are made, energy moves, and life changes follow.

SENSE YOUR HOME'S ENERGY

This exercise is designed to train you to perceive energy and its relationship to your physical self (aka your body) and your surroundings (namely, your home). To start, close your eyes and imagine walking across the threshold into your home. As you slowly envision yourself moving through each room, follow the prompts below.

1. Sense what your body does in response to each of your rooms. Do you feel yourself tensing up, or sinking into a state of relaxation? Do you get a knot in your stomach? Or a jolt of energy? You want to become very aware of your body's responses.

2. Now reflect on how those inner sensations correlate to specific feelings. Name these feelings, one by one, and acknowledge them without judgment. Is the energy of your home sustaining you? Answer as objectively as you can, which will help you perceive more.

When energy flows, the response is an expansive feeling in your body, a desire to move closer; a *no* response, by contrast, results in a pulling-away sensation, a contraction. It's that simple. In this book, I will guide you on many walks through your home and give you a chance to feel the nuances of your body's responses. Your *yes* and your *no* are the gateways to the more advanced skills of learning how to harness, direct, and solidify energy.

Four Ways to Recognize Energy Within the Home

How do your surroundings affect you on subconscious levels? What messages are the colors, the furnishings, the art, the objects in your home sending to your brain? The following are ways to think about elements in your home through the lens of energy to increase its flow.

1. Tension

The adage "opposites attract" isn't limited to romantic love. The energy created by opposing elements is potent in the home as well. Have you ever tried to bring together the negative and positive poles of two batteries to feel the energy created? It's palpable, right? You can deliberately create the same energy in your home when you want stimulation in your life. See for yourself: Try putting a rough brutalist sculpture on a prim lacquered sideboard. Or place a big, gestural, kooky plant in a very structured, minimalist living room. Or, as shown above, place a humble, rustic armoire in front of a refined geometric wallpaper. (For more examples of the tension of opposites, see pages 260–263.)

2. Color

Each of us has a visceral, emotive reaction to the energy inherent in different colors. Imagine entering an empty red room. How does your body respond? Your psyche? Now imagine how they would react upon entering the same room, only painted yellow. That difference in sensation as you imagine going back and forth between the two is the energy of color.

Some people need stimulation through intense, contrasting colors. Others with overwhelmed systems need soft colors to soothe them. Replicate this process for yourself by first identifying how you want to feel and then imagining standing in an empty room of a given color. Allow your body's responses to inform your choices. (For more on color, see page 252.)

3. Symbols

Look around. You are surrounded by more symbols than you realize. Symbols are the language of the unconscious in the same way that words are the language of the conscious. Think of your dreams, which are often inscrutable reflections of deep-seated aspects of the self. Make a list of the symbols in your home, along with any associations they form for you. This list is the energy you are telegraphing to your brain. Is it what you want to be feeding yourself?

Remember, where attention goes, energy flows. You also use symbols to shake up a long-term relationship with new energy, for example, to find a way out of inertia. (For more on the powerful energy of symbols, see page 108.)

4. Framing Devices

Each threshold in your home is a framing device: Seeing through it activates your attention. When you imagine a particular threshold, what is the first thing you see? Does it evoke a particular emotion? If so, is that what you want to be feeling? If not, how could you move things around to shift that feeling? Any wall you see beyond a doorway can be programmed to elicit an energy you want more of. If your combination of stuff isn't creating an inner *hell, yes!* as you enter the room, chances are you are not maximizing its potential. Overscale artwork, a plant on a pedestal, a sculptural chair, and bold color are my go-to choices when using framing devices to enhance beauty. (For more on framing devices, see pages 116–117.)

I designed this altar with the intention of calling forth the Future Self. The central figure represents the state of being I hope to access; the crystals amplify that energy. This is a meditation altar, but altars can also be secular (see page 58 for more on this).

The Future Is Present

As you continue to experiment within the realm of energy, you want to begin responding to the Future Self, which lies beyond the physical realm. It exists in the unmanifest as an energy channel with a greater receiving capacity than what you have now.

The Future Self isn't exactly in the future. Not in a linear sense, anyway. Rather, it is the realm of all possibility. You can access the feeling of Future Self energy in the here and now through your imagination, but it takes some practice. By learning to call this energy forth and anchor it to your current life on a spiritual, mental, emotional, and physical level, you are merging identities—present with future.

If you're new to this concept, take it slow and steady. When you focus too much on *How do I get there?* at the expense of *What does my Future Self feel like?* at this stage, confusion can set in. (*How do I get there?* tactics will be addressed in more detail in subsequent parts of this book.) Getting familiar with Future Self energy goes beyond a once-a-year peak spiritual experience that leaves you buzzing. Practice tuning in to it several times a day, as a meditation. I try to connect with my Future Self when I'm waiting in line at the supermarket, for example, or washing the dishes, or taking a break from work with tea in the afternoon. The best way I consistently connect with my Future Self is in the shower every morning, where I feel relaxed and unreachable. No cell phone, no disruptions. When I'm dialed in, the feeling often leads to moments of clarity or out-of-the-box thinking.

You can also use "outside markers" to get closer and closer to expanded inner sensations. These markers are soul-aligned desires: the thought of a career that matches your calling, deeper intimacy with your partner, achieving financial freedom, basking in a sense of belonging to a group of friends or peers. Breathe into the imagined feeling, then expand on it, feeling the pleasure of having it in your life *now*. Try it for one minute and see where you get. Focus on any bodily sensations and keep breathing, imagining yourself getting closer to that feeling. By tapping into it, you go beyond the range of where your present self lives and begin to tether to the Future Self.

How does this same energy relate to your home? The way you design your home can invoke the reality you want and, ultimately, help you experience fuller joy, fuller accomplishment, fuller satisfaction. This is how your home can serve as a conduit to the Future Self.

BECOME ONE WITH YOUR FUTURE SELF

Each of us has experienced the energy of the Future Self, whether or not we recognized it. Following are four ideas to help you become so intimate with your Future Self that it feels like a second skin. Practice getting into that vibration regularly.

1. Breathe into it. Sit down in a favorite comfortable spot. Take a few deep breaths, relaxing into your body a bit more with each long exhale. Close your eyes and tune in to what it feels like in your body when someone is falling in love with you and you are falling in love with them. Perceive yourself through the eyes of that person. Picture yourself standing there, being loved for who you are, at your most alive and vibrant. Notice the subtle electricity moving through your body as it flushes. That's it. The Future Self presents as an expanded state of being in love and turned on by life. Breathe into that feeling, imagining that it's a ball of positive energy that you are growing with each breath until it fills the whole room that you are in. Notice any bodily responses that accompany the sensation: goose bumps, tingling, warmth in your chest.

2. Write it. Give your Future Self a name (or use your own) and write about them as if they're living in the present moment. Find your perspective from a place that is believable to you yet still a stretch. Add details about what the Future Self's life looks and feels like. Scan your body and find four words to describe these feelings: *connected, grounded, calm, energized, dynamic, curious, fulfilled,* and so on. Print out these words and make multiple copies; fold them up and put them in places throughout the home where you are bound to notice them frequently. This is how you begin propagating Future Self energy like a seed and generating momentum.

3. Make it physical. I wear a bold, powerful, dynamic statement necklace whenever I want to feel the energy or a particular emotion of the Future Self. I also rely on power objects (see page 56) in my office: A glass bowl embodies the clarity and flow I aim to project in meetings. Other items placed on my bookshelf have more calm, balancing energy. When I look at them from my desk, I feel at ease.

Start placing objects of meaning at eye level, where you can engage with them daily. You are learning to interact with this new entity (the Future Self) more on the physical plane, not just in your head or your heart.

4. Make an altar to it. This can be spiritual (using crystals or talismans from a specific practice) or secular. Even two or three objects that resonate with the energy of your Future Self can work as an altar (for more on altars, see page 58). If possible, arrange one in the spot that you see from your bed when you wake up; any place that you stare at regularly when you're performing mundane tasks will also do. What's behind you in the mirror when you brush your teeth, for example, or in front of you when you wash dishes? As you look at the altar, practice recognizing the Future Self energy in your body.

Embodied Creation Is Next-Level Manifestation

Manifestation is an inside job: part art, part science, part practice, and part leap of faith. The more you engage with it, the more skill you develop, along with the capacity to use your mind, emotions, and the world around you to open yourself up to your highest intention. Manifestation means navigating yourself, step-by-step, in the direction you want to go. As you grow to understand your psyche and begin to see the beliefs on which it is built, you simultaneously hone your ability to manifest in every part of your life.

On one level, I love that current popular culture is mainstreaming ancient practices into manifestation. People are realizing how their words, thoughts, and emotions are reflections of internal processes that can affect their lives in the physical world. It is true. They do. This awareness alone may begin to shift your circumstances. However, the quick-fix, eyes-on-the-prize mentality of the pop culture approach to manifestation

can be counterproductive. If the result doesn't materialize quickly, people get frustrated and confused. They dismiss the process entirely, or allow a combination of self-shame and self-blame to set in before ultimately giving up.

In my experience, maintaining a high internal vibration to magnetize a high-vibration external life (which is the way manifestation is commonly understood, or at least how I learned to approach it) is untenable. I could maintain positive thoughts and happy vibes for only so long before I spiraled into anxiety, worry, and negative thinking. And then I blamed myself for having "counterproductive" feelings. Ouch; double whammy.

As transformational guide Jamila Reddy puts it, in manifestation "there's an overemphasis on the mental, the 'think positive' idea that if you change your thoughts, then your external circumstances will automatically improve as a result. Manifesting the car, for example, the job,

Your body can be deliberately reprogrammed to a higher vibration by your home, even when your thoughts and emotions are all over the place.

the partner, the vacation—is all external. People are missing the deep spiritual work."

Barbara Droubay, a somatic practitioner I work with extensively, agrees that most of us fall short of our goals because we don't really know how the process of manifestation works. "We cannot activate outside of our own selves. This is the crucial distinction between what is gently known as wishful thinking (or, more frustratingly, unrealized dreams) and true manifestation, which is embodied creation."

A key difference between manifestation and embodied creation is understanding the power of the physical world to affect your mental and emotional states. And wielding it deliberately to do so. Acknowledging that the physical world influences the internal world allows you to use your home to program thoughts, beliefs, and emotions into your body.

Your body can be deliberately reprogrammed to a higher vibration by your home, even when your thoughts and emotions are all over the place. Move your furniture around, your body responds. Paint your walls a different color, your body responds. Spend the weekend decluttering, your body responds. That body-home relationship is at the core of embodied creation. The results of these intentional energetic shifts are experienced and registered as powerful physical sensations.

The more you build on these positive bodily responses, the more they compound. When your home is aligned to the energy you want to embody in the *now*, it holds you, and in turn magnetizes the future. By nature of being physical, the home is much more consistent than your thoughts and emotions.

In Spatial Alchemy, beauty is a strategic tool you can learn to use for your spiritual, mental, and emotional growth. When you walk across the threshold of every room in your home and feel an inner *yes*, you will know you've created the positive magnetic current necessary for true embodied creation.

Power Objects

As you experiment with the art of taking energy into the physical world, the key is to build momentum incrementally. Begin with a power object or two and work from there. A power object is anything that symbolizes the energy you are aiming to embed in your life. Imagine it as a bridge for materializing the feeling of abundance. What item in your home physically represents this feeling for you?

A power object can be any piece that moves and motivates you. In the 1980s, "power suits" were all the rage, for example. By putting the suit on, the wearer assumed the identity of a business executive and leader. Wearing such suits day in and day out trained them to believe that they *were* that person, even if they didn't start out believing it. This is an example of using a physical object to expand your notion of who you are—and who you can become.

The most effective power objects are accessories, not furniture pieces or anything too weighty; you want to be able to play with the position and see where the item affects you the most. Begin by identifying items that hold rich, meaningful connections for you. Which feel the most in tune with the Future Self energy? Ask yourself which item that you already own you would choose to represent groundedness. Which item would you choose as a symbol of lightheartedness?

Now exalt your power object by placing it in a position of importance—on a mantel, on a shelf across from your bed, in the middle of your dining table, or on your desk. Use these objects as statement pieces, with plenty of negative space around them or centered between two identical objects. A power object can inspire the arrangement of everything around it, or it can stand on its own, commanding the space.

The next step is to interact with your power object and honor it as the representation of the more expanded you. Because one of my power objects is a pair of footed teal vases, I place dried or fresh branches in them and switch the branches out weekly (see page 73). This maintenance and attention to the objects encourages the energy of self-care, connection to nature, and growth.

By putting your attention on the expansion you want to materialize, you are feeding it and, in the process, cultivating a relationship with your abundant self. Eventually, you will tune your home to the "note" of this power object, as an orchestra tunes to the oboe. When you surround yourself with personal symbols of abundance, it becomes easier to anchor that feeling in your daily life.

After working with your power object for a week or two, assess if it still resonates. If not, try to find a different object (or buy something small that feels exquisite to you).

When my life started to feel like all work and no play, I chose a bold, artist-designed basketball as a power object. It reminds me that my creativity flourishes when I take a break and step away from my desk.

Altars

IF THE HEART OF THE HOME is the kitchen, then the womb of the home is the altar. Altars are designed to expand your focus, to help you arrive at a wider awareness, and to bring clarity and direction. Spiritual altars often hold crystals, figurines of deities, and incense, but there are no set rules. Select objects that feel in harmony with your soul. Lean in to whatever it is you are seeking more of—beauty, peace, nature, intuition, kindness.

Every surface in your home is an opportunity to make a secular altar that serves as a bridge to who you are becoming. Secular altars don't have to look like altars to anyone but yourself. To everyone else, they may resemble beautifully styled vignettes. For you, they serve as very practical, purposeful spaces, where you can take your vision board off the cloud and pull it into physical form.

Look around to find space for an altar (or more than one) within your home. I like to place a large object in the center of my altar and frame it with a pair of items (like statement candlesticks) in a triangular arrangement. Symmetrical pairs heighten the energy of whatever they surround, and regularly lighting the candles sparks your intention. (In spiritual traditions around the globe, fire is a symbol of transformation and reverence.)

Continue to play with the display until you get that "in sync" feeling. There is no right or wrong. Trust your gut.

Finally, keep your altar tidy. Interact with it frequently, swapping items in and out. I use trays to keep altars dynamic, and I switch up mine once a season to keep the energy fresh. The more you interact with your altar, the better you can focus on your life vision.

No one would guess that these bookshelves are an altar, but taking a cue from my basketball power object (see page 56), I intentionally styled them to call forth a playful, transportive energy.

Transcending Taste

When we talk about home design, too often we limit the conversation to the subject of taste, in a binary way—it's either good or bad. From this perspective, "good" taste becomes exclusive rather than inclusive. Something you're expected to live up to. Also, in that belief system, taste applies only to the visual sense. It stays where you can see it, on the physical surface, but neglects to address the spiritual, mental, and emotional realms.

Because taste is centered in comparison, it is inherently hierarchical, setting up a dynamic that feeds the ego more than the soul. In Spatial Alchemy, we shift the focus to what each of us is truly born with in equal measure: self-expression. Expanding the notion of taste beyond the good vs. bad relationship and into the creational and psychological depths allows you to access your full potential. You begin to connect with your psyche, your brain, your heart, and your body, and use each of them to transform your home into your life laboratory.

Once you start this archaeological dig into your soul, on a Socratic quest to know thyself, you turn the notion of taste on its head. This brings your intuition to the fore, where you can bulk it up, like a muscle.

Picture the topsoil. That's surface-level taste. To grow roots, you need to go deeper. So imagine taste as a pathway to this something deeper, hitting the emotional and mental levels as it makes its way all the way down to the spiritual level, where intuition and identity converge.

By examining taste on the full spectrum, we can learn to achieve what we want—freedom and fulfillment in our aesthetic decisions—and overthrow the oppressive weight of collective notions. That's because choosing objects based on an external idea of taste silences the inner voice. You are tuning in to the wrong frequency, in direct contrast to the foundation of Spatial Alchemy: As within, so without.

Your identity as expressed through your personal style choices is malleable. As you begin to play with identity (beginning on page 104) and focus on what you believe you deserve, your self-expression begins to morph and to widen.

Used deliberately and with skill, self-expression is a remarkable tool. To access it, begin by examining taste as identity on every level. Start at the core, and you'll understand that great design and cohesive personal expression involve taking risks, as does committing to a partner, pivoting to a new career, or making other bold but uncertain moves. Materializing your dreams is nothing more than thickening energy into matter. When you approach your home with this intention, you follow your gut and open your heart to the possibilities, transcending taste to create a beautiful, one-of-a-kind home that reflects your true being.

COGNITIVE DISSONANCE
AND DESIGN CHOICES

Why do so many of us adopt the taste of others rather than develop our own? According to Tom Vanderbilt, author of *You May Also Like: Taste in an Age of Endless Choice*, our decisions are often related to cognitive dissonance. The term was defined by Leon Festinger, an American psychologist, in the 1950s. Through his work on cognitive dissonance and social comparison, Festinger theorized that when we feel psychologically uncomfortable, we immediately want to reduce that dissonance and return to consonance. Today, we might call that our safe space or comfort zone. We retreat to choices that help us avoid dissonance and any decisions that might let discomfort creep in. It is very uncomfortable, even disarming, to stand out from the pack we identify with, so we stay in our self-enforced "lanes."

Fear of cognitive dissonance helps explain why we are hardwired to make familiar choices on all aesthetic levels and in particular in our homes. Many of us stick to the path of least resistance—secure, but unable to access a level of energy that leads us to growth. We don't trust our own instincts and end up making choices that are more in line with what's trendy than what we are truly yearning for. This is because we need to teach ourselves how to translate our soul desires into the physical world, to transform that energy into matter. Oftentimes, our home design is more informed by default past identities than the deliberate calling in of what we want to experience and how we want to live.

Moving from Default
to Deliberate Design

After many years of working in interiors, I've come to realize that most people just want to feel good in their homes. They don't care about trends, but they get so overwhelmed by all the options—furniture, styles, colors, artwork, and more—that they freeze in place. Because they are afraid of getting it wrong, they avoid deliberate decision-making and stay stuck in default mode, choosing to mimic other people's examples. Spatial Alchemy is designed to help folks move beyond this state of indecision.

What makes deliberate design work? It starts with declaring your intention. As soon as you do so, sparks fly. Decorating decisions no longer seem isolated or disconnected. Instead, each choice becomes part of a dynamic whole. Nothing is haphazard because the vision is cohesive and purposeful; everything is added willingly. Little by little, you walk yourself beyond the roadblocks that keep you in design limbo.

Think of deliberate design in terms of technology. You are writing new code for updated programs. First, you want to remove any glitches. Before you can begin to imagine how you want to transform your home, you must strip things down to the essentials, to remove anything that no longer resonates. (We'll get to this dissolving process in more detail on page 76.) Finally, you'll find a way to embed your intentions clearly and meaningfully in the objects that remain, diving into your personal attachment to them and the narratives they deliver. Ultimately, the goal of improving the product (in this case, the home) is to enhance the user experience

Having great style is not enough. But mix it with self-awareness, and you've got gold.

of it. And the user is you. The result is an entire *system* upgrade, of your living space and your life.

To extend the home-as-product metaphor a bit further, you could choose to fall back on "preloaded" design choices—a dining room set with matching table and chairs, maybe, or bedding that's bundled in one bag rather than handpicked and layered, piece by piece. Though convenient, this approach to design decision-making omits intention from the equation. By avoiding meaningful choices, you limit mental or emotional connections, which are key to cultivating a truly magical, deeply personal relationship with your home.

Having great style is not enough. But mix it with self-awareness, and you've got gold. The act of picking and choosing for yourself is self-affirming. Each decision

represents a vision that's unique to you. Slowly but oh so surely, you compose a suite of design features that work together organically, harmoniously, and seamlessly.

And just like that, you evolve along with the space that surrounds you. Your approach to home design is both more confident and more forgiving because you can turn design *mistakes* into design *statements*. This encourages a continual upleveling of confidence.

Going from operating in default mode to being deliberate—using psychology, intentionality, and style—is how you will materialize your inner vision.

63

My intention in designing our powder room was to solidify four energetic qualities I was seeking: gutsiness, strength, earthiness, and sensuality. The strong wood details, black-glazed clay tiles, and dim lighting combine to help get me there.

STATE YOUR INTENTIONS FOR YOUR HOME

Intention is the direction in which you consciously steer yourself. Stating the specifics of your desires gives you clarity and precision. The following exercise is designed to help you clarify the reality you want to create, merge with it, and make decisions. The questions are inspired by similar ones developed by life coach Brooke Castillo, whose work has had a big influence on me. Use a pen and paper to record your responses.

1. Be still and close your eyes. Take a deep breath. Walk toward a mirror hanging in your home. Begin to see your image looking back at you. This is your Future Self. Gaze into their eyes and sense the difference between the energy in their body and the energy in yours. How is your Future Self feeling? Once you've tracked the difference between those feelings and yours, aim to try to lessen the gap, so that eventually you become a mirror, reflecting back the open energy of the Future Self.

2. Now envision yourself stepping through the mirror toward the Future Self and merging with it. You and your Future Self are one. Open your eyes, and see yourself walking up to the home of the Future Self—the best version of the home you currently live in.

3. What energy does the Future Self possess that you want to invite into your life? Name four energetic qualities of the Future Self that you want to solidify in your current home.

4. As you're moving through your home in the weeks ahead, notice the items that are not in resonance with these four words. How do these items make you feel? Are these feelings you would choose for yourself? Would you buy this item again? Going forward, practice seeing your home through the eyes of the Future Self more frequently. Each time you do, your observations will get more nuanced and meaningful.

DISSOLVING PAST SELVES

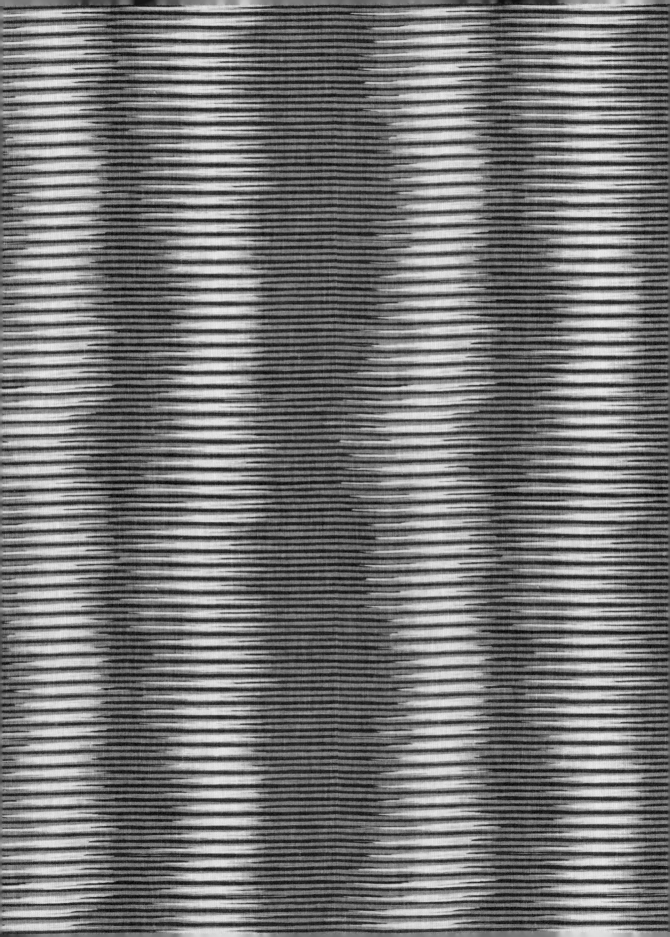

Shedding old identities means you can plant and cultivate new ones.

In Part One, you learned how the energy of your home affects your psyche and can encourage you to tap into the expanded energy of your Future Self. Now, in Part Two, the objective is to recognize outdated identities in your home, one by one, as part of a concrete, logical process.

Many of us are so mired in our subjective viewpoints that we become myopic. With practice, however, you can hone your ability to see yourself through the objective lens, with the eyes of a gentle observer. In school, we learn the skills of logical problem-solving. Here, you will be encouraged to rely on those same skills to observe the connection between your identity and your home to locate default patterns at work.

Our perceived identities, (possibly) outdated conditioning, judgments, and self-worth settings all contribute to the ways in which we design our homes. They continually inform our choices, consciously or unconsciously. When you see your undesirable patterns neutrally, however, without shame or blame, you can release them and make space for new thoughts, new behaviors, new habits.

This exercise of releasing and replacing mirrors the alchemical process of *solve et coagula*, Latin for "dissolve and coagulate." We are dissolving patterns of identity that no longer ring true. (Remember, identity is not fixed. It is made up of layers, more like an onion than a potato.) Next, we are establishing a feedback loop between you and the new templates you want to reinforce, using the physical world to pull the Future Self into the present moment.

Our focus in this part of the book is to discover where your home lacks coherence with that Future Self. The dissolving and rebuilding process, which is the essence of Spatial Alchemy, begins with unpacking your belief systems and identifying how those beliefs manifest in your home environment. Coagulating spirit into matter in this way, as an expanded vibration, may feel uncomfortable. The biggest obstacle often lies in your thoughts: what you believe you deserve, what you grant yourself permission to have, and how you project your self-worth.

The only requirement is that you dig deep to identify and disrupt your long-held patterns. In turn, you will witness how the process of altering the physical world corresponds to conscious shifts in your mindset. When you begin to give yourself what you want in your home, you generate the momentum required for it to appear in the outside world, too.

On the following pages, you will learn:

- How your beliefs create your home by calcifying specific psychological patterns in your stuff

- How to break outdated, negative patterns as well as those that feel significantly off course

- How to stretch into expanded self-worth through your home

- How to deliberately create space to welcome new energy into your life

Who Do You Think You Are?

Self-worth is nothing more than your belief system. Kathryn Morrison has made this realization her life's work. As a mindset and personal growth coach, she helps clients see unlimited potential in themselves, uncover what's keeping them from achieving their stated goals, and generate momentum toward self-fulfillment. In order to shift your mindset, she believes, you must begin by identifying your own self-imposed rules or deeply held beliefs and asking yourself if you really want to hang on to them. "This is how you start to track what's holding you back from getting what you want," Morrison says. "Ask yourself what becomes possible when you get beneath the limiting thoughts. What would the difference in your perspective look like?"

Any change in your thinking involves being open and willing to step back and see yourself clearly. If you have a goal in mind but don't think you can ever achieve it, ask yourself why not. Why *can't* you have the home you want? Maybe, you tell yourself, it's because you have small children, or pets. Or maybe you are in a rental and are waiting until you have more money or a better job or have moved into your "forever home." You may tell yourself any number of things to keep from realizing the life you want to live. Walk yourself back from those self-doubts and keep pulling the thread. As Morrison says, "You have to get at the conditioned beliefs that lie under the mindset until you get to *Wait, none of this is true, but I'm sitting here telling myself this untruth. I don't want to believe that untruth anymore.* Only then can you start to let go, change the mindset, and take action."

That's not to say the process is easy! Our ways of thinking have been firmly ingrained in us, and we move forward by seeing, questioning, and removing the mental blockages, many of which are long-standing. This requires the fortitude and will to get out of your own way.

Remember: You control the story that you tell yourself and others. Instead of judging yourself as not good enough, flip the script. The decision is yours, ultimately. Morrison often reminds clients that the root of the word *decide* is "to cut." "It literally means to cut off all other options," she says. "This is a 'no going back' moment! You would only be going back to the static and stagnant energy."

Ask yourself: *What am I waiting for?*

Does your artwork represent current identities that you want to reinforce, or outdated ones that you are ready to release? A grid of zodiac symbols, for example, offers an opportunity to consider why we hold on to established ideas of ourselves, whether or not they ring true.

Promoting Myself

In the five-year span represented in these photos, you can see how the design of my home offices not only represented distinct phases in my career, but also my evolving relationships to purpose, money, and entrepreneurship. In that time, after many years as a stylist, my intention was to step into something more expansive and aligned with my soul, so I continually refined my surroundings to call forth the businessperson I longed to be.

Fig. 1 Boxed In

This office was situated in the poorly lit rec room of my condo, with the desk facing a wall and a lamp that, while chic, didn't provide adequate lighting. Looking back, this was a living representation of the career confusion I was experiencing—it felt as if I were groping around in the dark. The blue artwork was a prop from a photo shoot, which left me staring at a representation of the career I was longing to leave. And I tried to soften the unwelcoming plastic office chair with a sheepskin, but it never felt comfortable. I was not considering the way my body was held, and whether the office chair, or "work throne," was aligned with where I was hoping to carry myself.

Fig. 2 Let It Go

At this point in my office evolution, my family and I were in our rental home, and my career had undergone a big shift, catalyzed by the pandemic. My inner sense of overwhelm was mirrored by my choice to work on a funky, surrealist-inspired table, which I designed. Eight years later, its many different, thin, and haphazardly placed legs were reinforcing the scattered identity I was hoping to leave behind. For sentimental reasons, I resisted letting the table go, and hung on to it even though it represented the opposite of the clear focus and support I was craving. The setup was positioned so that I could look out at the green lawn, but this meant my back was to the door—not a powerful position for an entrepreneur who longed to feel in charge of her growing business.

Fig. 3 Who's the Boss?

In this newly reconfigured office, created as I was looking to take my interiors coaching business to the next level, my furniture choices were daring and audacious—by design. I chose a grand desk that helped me feel grounded and stable in my career and a chair that felt regal. Then I accessorized them with chic, fancy pieces that were slightly over my budget, including a leather desk blotter straight out of a successful Madison Avenue boss lady's corner office. Many of these decisions were out of my comfort zone—I wasn't familiar with the kind of person who would work in an office like this. But that was the point. I persevered, incorporating other small styling elements (like a brass stapler and a pair of crystal paperweights) that felt like a stretch. In the end, these decorating decisions combined to anchor me to my career intentions while also expanding my vision of my business self.

Fig. 1

Fig. 2

Fig. 3

Mirrors

MANY PEOPLE STAND IN FRONT OF THE MIRROR and
look at how they are dressed, whether their hair looks
good, and so on, but they don't take the time to fully *see*
themselves. When you decide to put yourself on a clear
and specific transformational trajectory, seeing yourself is
imperative. Making intentional choices about the mirror
you are using will enable you to see beyond the surface
image and use the mirror as a tool to consciously reflect
who you are becoming back to yourself.

Take full-length mirrors, as an example: Most people
have at least one, but for many, it's an inexpensive
hardware-store version hanging on the back of a door.
Is this congruent with how you want to see your full self
and who you want to become? Consider the cumulative
difference between looking at yourself in a "default"
mirror every day for a year, and then imagine doing
the same with one chosen intentionally to create an
emotional and mental charge. You are programming self-
worth through your choice of mirror.

The placement of mirrors is also impactful. Think
of where you want to see yourself, and how the mirror
relates to the interior setting. One of the first things I do
when working with a client is take mirrors off the backs of
doors and relocate them to more prominent positions.
For example, putting a large-scale mirror at the end of
a long hallway creates a potent dynamic when you walk
toward yourself daily. Having a full-length mirror greet
you right as you walk into your foyer helps you reset
and transition from outside to inside. If your bathroom
is big enough, hanging a full-length mirror in it can help
support the goal of accepting and loving your body.

Fig. 1

Fig. 2

Fig. 3

Fig. 4

Fig. 1 *To bring order to a cluttered mind, offer much-needed structure via a mirror with a faceted frame.* ***Fig. 2*** *To activate expansion in your life, place a bold, overscale mirror in a prominent position.* ***Fig. 3*** *The romantic, fairy-tale quality of this Venetian-style mirror is heightened by the dramatic, ceiling-height curtains that surround it.* ***Fig. 4*** *Placing two mirrors across from each other helps bounce light around a small space, and lets you see yourself from multiple angles.*

Spatial Alchemy & *Solve et Coagula*

The concept of *solve et coagula* ("dissolve and coagulate" in Latin) forms the backbone of alchemy—both the medieval practice and Spatial Alchemy. (It also happens to be a bedrock of modern chemistry.) In a nutshell, *solve et coagula* allows you to transform one substance into another, as the ancients did; first you dissolve (*solve*) what no longer serves you, and then you solidify (*coagula*) that which does.

According to this ancient practice, you cannot elevate something without first examining its composition. Alchemy is not simply a matter of "Out with the old, in with the new." Instead, the directive is to take it apart, examine its essence, and build back a more exquisite new version.

When you view your home as an alchemist, the matter at hand consists of self-worth settings, outdated identities, and default patterns, all of which underlie and form the programs that run your home, and in the process may limit your potential. By dissolving these codes, all of which are embedded in your daily surroundings, you are free to put energy into new and improved programs rather than self-defeating ones.

To dissolve and coagulate is to create a new personal narrative, with your home as its physical expression. When I walk into any home, I sense where things are tied more to the past than the present. I focus on items that represent old belief systems. Most clients express what they want at our first meeting, but they may not see how existing patterns in their home are holding them back. The homes don't reflect the way the client says they want to feel. To bring their surroundings into alignment and resonance, we start with a releasing process before we even begin talking about buying anything.

In broad strokes, here's how the *solve et coagula* process works to upgrade your system. First, identify and study your patterns. Next, you want to release any outdated codes. Once you've articulated the energy you want to seed, you can begin to plant and cultivate it. Finally, solidify your new identity by embedding items throughout your home that foster its growth.

1.

IDENTIFY

2.

RELEASE

3.

SEED

4.

SOLIDIFY

From Scarcity to Abundance

Once I began studying my patterns with regularity, I realized that I was being held back by an unconscious scarcity identity. This belief system convinced me that I lacked options, causing me to settle for less, and was no doubt left over from my days as a child refugee from the former Soviet Union, assimilating into the United States and consistently feeling like a "have-not." As a result, I allowed myself to be resigned to my "fate" rather than resolved to change it. I had no idea how entrenched this mindset was until I looked around my home and saw the patterning everywhere, mostly in the things I surrounded myself with, like castaway objects that I brought home by default (often from photo shoots). If something was offered to me for free, I took it, even if it didn't align with what I desired. Who was I to say no?

When you want to create a deliberate identity, it helps to understand how belief systems work. Take scarcity vs. abundance: This mindset doesn't require the physical existence of either. Abundance refers to the feeling of having more than enough of something, not necessarily wealth. When you are satiated, you feel abundant. So much so that you can be generous. Whether you want more abundance in time, love, creativity, self-worth, or money, the mechanics of identity-shifting are the same.

Making more space for abundance starts with your mindset. When you intentionally program more abundance into the physical environment of your home, you increase your momentum toward it. How do you step into the identity of abundance when you aren't currently feeling that way? Begin by deactivating layers of scarcity that you no longer want to feed and bolstering nascent layers of abundance that you do. Along the way, it's essential to take note of the effects.

When you intentionally program more abundance into the physical environment of your home, you increase your momentum toward it.

The home of one of my clients, Natasha, was filled with hand-me-downs and thrift-store finds. She was a highly successful executive in her fifties, and yet her furniture had all been acquired when she was in her thirties. She wasn't seeing how attached she was to this scrappy version of herself, and how a scarcity mindset still controlled much of the decision-making when it came to decorating her home. In fact, the mindset was so pervasive that she wasn't allowing herself to live inside the abundance she was earning.

Each time I identified a piece that could be replaced or upgraded, she pushed back. "This item is so functional," she'd say. "Why would I get rid of it?" When we are letting go of outdated identities, there is always resistance. Listen to that voice in your head: What is it saying to you? Does it feel like it comes from a place of scarcity disguised as practicality?

After acknowledging the roots of her hesitation, Natasha decided she wanted to work toward the mindset of abundance. Slowly she began to release the items that made her feel the worst. Out went two armchairs that looked fine in the room but reminded her of the ex-boyfriend with whom she thrifted them back in the day. Their absence made her realize how heavy his presence had actually felt in the room. Next, she let go of a rickety side table she'd always liked the look of. She was beginning to see the symbolism in these items she had been clinging to. Once she began to experience the spaciousness on the other side of these releases, she was able to gain momentum naturally and acknowledge how the shifts in the home created shifts in her mindset.

After about six weeks of releasing one item at a time, the lake house she had long been searching for finally came on the market. Releasing scarcity in one home opened the door to her dream home.

WELCOME ABUNDANCE

Scarcity lives inside the "I don't have enough" expressions, whether or not they are even consciously expressed. Often, it's hard to untangle that sentiment from life experiences that are mirroring it right back at you. You may think, *Well, clearly, I don't have enough space. My apartment is teeny, so I am just stating facts.* This is where we humans get stuck in a thought loop. One of the most efficient ways I have found to dislodge myself from the *I don't have enough* quagmire is to plant "sufficiency" into my home. To examine your relationship with the scarcity–abundance spectrum and disrupt patterns, look around and consider the following questions:

– Where tdoes the belief *I don't have enough money* live in your belongings? These are things you settled for, that never felt like you in the first place. Maybe they were in a clearance sale, or were given to you, or you told yourself you would live with them temporarily, just until you could afford something nicer. Take note of how they make you feel. The ones you feel worst about are your first candidates to release.

– Where does *I don't have enough time* live? These are the things you put off addressing because you don't think you can deal with them now, but you never seem to make time to do so. You keep playing the game of kick the can, reinforcing the belief without solving for it. Set an intention to make the time. Start by scheduling twenty minutes twice a week to work on your home.

– Where does *I don't have enough space* live? This is when things are piled up on top of each other, or crammed into tight areas, and you haven't come up with solutions to the problem. You've been sitting with the complaint about space constraints and not facing the reality of them. This reinforces the complaint rather than frees it.

– Where does *I don't have enough confidence* live? This is where you don't want to make bold moves or statements for fear of making mistakes. You play it safe in your design decisions, like choosing bitsy items or neutral colors because you're afraid of going bold. What else do you feel you don't have enough of? Where does that feeling live in your home?

Now examine where your ideas about abundance live. Look around and consider the following questions:

– Where does the belief *I feel whole* live? You feel as if your space is unified, and furniture pieces are in conversation with one another. All the colors feel coherent. This doesn't have to be a whole room; even a sliver of a room works as a template to replicate.

– Where does *I celebrate* live? The more you make space for joy, the more you have to celebrate, which is gratitude in action. As a practice, celebration extends your self-worth. Most of us celebrate holidays but not small personal achievements and beginnings. What celebratory rituals do you have, and how often do you engage in them? Where do you celebrate at home, and what items do you use? Can you expand on these rituals in a way that feels authentic?

– Where does *I feel creative* live? Where does your home already sparkle with your creativity? What space makes you smile when you see it because it is so *you*? Take note of what you did right. Is it the colors, the shapes, the unusual mix of things that you love? Often, we focus so much on where we are stuck that we don't give equal weight to where our creativity is flowing.

– Where does *I can slow down* live? In our nonstop digital age, we need to teach ourselves how to stop without crashing. I learned this the hard way, through burnout. What parts of your home encourage you to move at a slower pace? Note all the gentle, soft areas of your home (the "yin," in Eastern philosophy). If you want more slowness in your life, begin expanding these spaces (and pay close attention to the passive energy section, beginning on page 183).

Where else do you feel you have abundance in your life? Where does that abundance live in your home? Answering these questions will bring clarity and direction to the dissolving step.

Identifying Common Patterns at Work

Like scarcity and abundance, other duality patterns exist in your home. Neither side is all positive or all negative, but if you lean too far toward one end of the spectrum for your comfort, your home will reflect this imbalance. The following list includes common pairs of mindset patterning as they relate to the home. Ask yourself where you fall on each spectrum and if this pattern is serving you. Those who lean heavily toward one side sometimes judge the other side as wrong. Take note of your judgments, which may be preventing you from creating balance in your life.

Comfort / Style

This one comes down to how much you want your home to look good and how much you want to sink into it, and whether that balance serves your larger intention.

Mentally scan your home, noticing if, in some places, a strong preference for a "cool factor" could be negatively affecting your body. Did you choose your sofa based on how it looks, without sitting on it? Are you happy with how it feels when you do? Many of those shapely sofas in design magazines look great because they photograph well. But fewer hold your body in a way that's truly nurturing, as if you're being embraced. If you have some sculptural upholstered pieces, balance those hard edges with other, more comfy furniture.

Conversely, too much overstuffed upholstered furniture can look heavy and unkempt, telegraphing inertia. The antidote to the "sweatpants salon" is to swap out a few items for sculptural pieces.

Spontaneous / Cautious

Design freeze is a mental state. Too much caution speaks to fear of failure, which keeps you in limbo. The antidote lies in stepping into a spontaneous mindset, allowing decisions to be less weighty, not so serious. As a bold but low-commitment move, paint one wall of a bathroom a bright color and see how it feels.

Unbalanced spontaneity, by contrast, can result in regret and guilt. Do you frequently have buyer's remorse? Do you go with your gut rather than thinking things through? Keep in mind that many design "mistakes" can be salvaged and even used to your advantage. Get creative with your solutions. For example, temper an overstuffed, ginormous sofa (often the most costly and unreturnable design misstep) with patterned wallpaper that speaks "louder" than the furniture. If you fall within this spectrum, practice not buying anything until you've done a round or two of *solve* (page 94) to be able to lean in to new mindsets.

Rule Bender / Rule Follower

Do you define yourself by your dare-to-be-different iconoclasm, always trying to make a big statement? Or are you more likely to follow a well-trodden path?

For years, the rebel identity ran strong in me. I put rule benders on a pedestal while judging rule followers as weak. This pattern was everywhere in my home, which was filled with too many "out there" objects vying for attention. If you, too, favor rule bending, be aware of how many strong design statements are present in your home, and whether they are working in harmony or drowning one another out. Integrating a few quiet, timeless, classic pieces allows quirkier elements more opportunity to shine.

On the flip side, if most of your decor is matchy-matchy or nondescript, guided by easy "can't go wrong" choices seen on social media, try something bold to consciously balance your individual voice with "the way everyone else does it" approach. Take a leap with small stuff first, to gain confidence—a custom lampshade is an easy first move.

Minimalist / Maximalist

There are those who need a home filled with copious accessories to feel inner safety, but the tendency to hold on to stuff also correlates to clinging to the past. Meanwhile, others live to let go—sometimes too much for their own comfort. They feel constricted and weighed down by stuff, as if it's impeding their freedom.

Wherever you fall on the spectrum, balance your tendency with its opposite. When you design your home too minimally, you won't feel held or embraced by it. Harmonize empty space with the energy of warmth, in small increments. If you favor maximalism, try breaking up the bulk of your stuff. Look at the negative space itself as a shape, and see what shapes are created by separating those forms with some much-needed breathing room.

IDENTIFY YOUR PATTERNS

Negative belief systems create patterns that take actual form in the way you live. To see these beliefs, you must cultivate an objective lens that lets you perceive your home through a stranger's eyes. Start by conducting a completely neutral assessment to gain intel without emotion or self-judgment. Are there things in your home that you are holding on to even though they're holding you back? These physical objects may be keeping a reality in place that you are ready to shed. Here's how to get started:

1. Leave the house. Shake yourself out. Do ten jumping jacks. Then, reenter your home. As you walk through the doorway, ask yourself: If I were a visitor seeing my home for the first time, what are the first things I would notice?

2. Slowly move from room to room. In each one, imagine you are seeing the home for the first time and feel your body respond. What parts of the room expand your body with a *yes* response or contract your body with a resounding *no*? Next, ask yourself:

– Is the room inviting?

– Does the room soothe my nervous system, or overwhelm it?

– Is each area of the room, including corners, actively used?

– Does it have adequate storage?

3. Identify positive aspects of your home. What do you appreciate most about it, and what choices inform that satisfaction? Where does the space feel set up with everyone's needs and comforts in mind? What rooms make you feel good? Where do you go when you need to feel soothed?

4. Now focus on potential problem areas. Are there parts of the room that seem to be neglected? Does anything obstruct easy passage around the space? Is anything broken or obsolete?

5. Notice recurring patterns that emerge. If you don't immediately spot any, go from room to room and start looking at objects one at a time, asking whether your Future Self might own any of them.

After you've completed your tour, reflect on your answers. Try to identify correlations between pain points in your home and those in your life. Your goal is to perceive the level of self-worth you've coded into your space, without judgment. Give yourself credit for all the good design decisions you've made! You want to lean in to what's working in your home and see where you can bring more of that to the rest of the space. When it comes to the problem areas you identified, what beliefs informed those design decisions? Do they represent deliberate choices, or default ones? How do the areas of neglect in your home relate to your own self-care? Are you neglecting yourself?

When I first did this exercise, I finally saw how neglected the basement of my rental home was. The mechanical equipment had not been properly cared for in years. There were spiderwebs in the corners. Because this was not the "pretty" part of the house, I hadn't prioritized it. Once I recognized the issue, I saw how I tend to neglect the practical stuff not only in utilitarian spaces but also in many other areas of my life, preferring to focus on beauty. (A job hazard for a stylist, for sure.)

Keep in mind that this is not a one-time exercise. It's unlikely that anyone will identify all of their problematic patterns in just one round. Take the process slowly, and avoid putting pressure on yourself. You will uncover deeper layers with each new pass and may notice things that you've practiced not seeing. That's the point: to retrain your eye to see clearly, since we are usually mired in our everyday habits. In the case of my basement, I set aside four thirty-minute blocks of time within a two-week span to clean surfaces and group similar things into lidded baskets. This gave me the momentum I needed to tackle the more unpleasant job of crawling into corners to clean them. The pleasure I got at the end of this process led to a decrease in stress and the resolve to repeat this exercise regularly.

SCALING UP

KRISTINA IS A MINDSET COACH, and a daring, super-confident individual by nature. This wasn't always reflected in her home, however, where she played small by default in her office. The walls were filled with tiny pictures that seemed out of step with the boldness of her character, especially in her Zoom space, where she conducts the bulk of her online business. When I pointed this out, she immediately recognized an unconscious pattern left over from a former more controlled and less expressive identity. She recognized how the little framed pics were a reflection of this old identity: small, safe, cute.

As an antidote, I encouraged her to replace the tiny photos with one big gesture, an oversize painting that made a statement more aligned with her spirit. As a business coach, she understood the power of having her backdrop frame her with a high level of gravitas. Rather than buying something generic, she commissioned an abstract piece from a local artist—a huge, energetic burst of color. The swap of a large piece of art for many small ones provided dynamic tension and a counterbalance to the items on Kristina's desk that were small by necessity—the pencil sharpener, pen holder, binder clips, and so on. She bought a chic and sturdy desk with thick, solid legs that embodied the solid, stable energy she wanted to project as the founder of her business, and let go of the sentimental but scrawny table she had been using, which lacked storage. In doing so, she set up her office to signal (consciously and unconsciously) whom she wanted to become and the direction in which she wanted her business to grow.

We moved the small framed art into Kristina's newly renovated bathroom, where the scale of the images is more in line with that of the space. They no longer feel puny. Now, throughout the home, there is more agreement between Kristina's surroundings and her self-worth, and as a result, her online business has quickly grown exponentially.

Tripping Hazards

When you are repeating an action day in and day out and something is getting in the way of easeful movement, you are coming face-to-face with tripping hazards.

Tripping hazards live in your daily nuisances. Some are the result of organizing issues, or space issues, or time issues, or design issues. Many are a combination of all of the above. These small annoyances may seem so insignificant that you ignore them, which is easier than addressing them head-on. Or so you think. You tell yourself that it'll take too much energy, or time, or money to fix them. You'd rather just move on with your day, annoyances and all.

The most obvious examples are the literal ones: Maybe there's a corner of a rug that you trip over almost every day. I had a client who did that for months after moving into a new home, rather than simply taping down the rug or moving it. It wasn't quite symmetrical to her bed, so it got in her way every morning and night. She was so focused on her to-do list that the small stumbles didn't ever register as a problem.

After our first session, I suggested moving the rug. A few days later, she reported back. She couldn't believe how much better she felt now that she wasn't tripping. She had avoided a very easy fix because she was focusing her attention on big-picture moves.

Many of us have similar tripping hazards in our homes, the result of neglecting ourselves for the sake of busyness. Where are you ignoring yourself? It may not be obvious or something you consider a big deal.

Spend a day pinpointing your tripping hazards, and you might be amused by what you find. Eliminating them usually doesn't take much effort, yet you will likely feel an immediate uptick of energy and pride once you finally do, and a resolve to address them more often going forward.

Beyond literally tripping, all kinds of hazards exist. In the kitchen, this means being unable to find the spices you need while you're cooking. The labels may be impossible to read because of your storage setup, requiring you to sort through countless jars to find the one you want. Set aside time to get bigger, clearer labels; make more room by throwing away spices that are past their prime; or simply move the spices to a spot where the labels are easy to read and the jars are accessible.

In utility spaces, you may be continually storing objects in the wrong place. Imagine a hair dryer in your bathroom that falls out whenever you open a tall cabinet. Maybe it even hits you on the head from time to time. The solution might be to add a hook within the cabinet from which to hang it, or to buy a bin with a tight-fitting lid to hold it, or to move it to a lower shelf. None of these solutions should take more than a few minutes.

In the bedroom, the hazard might be a nightstand with no space for your bedtime essentials. If you need to keep getting up to retrieve something, like a glass of water or your book and eyeglasses, *after* you've settled in, you are not giving yourself the experience of sinking in. Same goes for easy chairs in the living room, where you may not have a landing spot for a cup of tea or a way to adjust a reading light, and so on.

TIME ON YOUR SIDE

Here's a little secret about tripping hazards: Most are solved in twenty minutes or less. (If one can't be dealt with in an hour, then it's a bigger issue; it may require rethinking or redesigning a whole room.)

You'd be amazed how quickly the problems you "don't have time to fix" can be remedied. Try setting a timer as a test. Everyone has twenty minutes to deal with something. I do this all the time, and I enlist my partner as my accountability buddy. Generally, I am able to remove the tripping hazard in this time frame or devise a practical solution for fixing it soon. Getting myself to do that is a chore, but the dopamine hit my brain gets when I'm finished is worth the effort every time.

BODY CHOREOGRAPHY

The way you treat your body is a hallmark of your self-worth. Programming physical ease and pleasure into your home is the epitome of caring for your body. To understand this mind-body connection and how you optimize it, study the choreography of your body as you move through your home. Track your daily movements and consider the following questions:

– Pay close attention to anything that stands in your way or impedes your movements. What's keeping you from taking the most direct path from point A to point B, for example? If there are items that obstruct you, why haven't you moved them out of the way to a more logical place?

– How does the way you've arranged furnishings help you move more gracefully? For example, is a floor lamp between two rooms forcing you to walk around it every time you pass by?

– Are lamps within easy reach when you need them? Do you need to get out of bed to turn the light on or off in the bedroom, for example? Some folks have apps that do that, and I can only imagine the level of self-love they show themselves when they use one.

– Notice where cords are located. Are they blocking pathways? Are phone and other electronic chargers hard to reach?

– Where are the nicest views in your home? Is there a comfortable chair or other good vantage point from which to enjoy them?

– Look at your storage systems, including cabinets, drawers, bins, and the like. Are they easy to access?

When your body consistently registers frustration and obstruction in your movements, your brain gets the signal that you are microdosing annoyance. By making intentional adjustments to these irritants, you systematically teach yourself to remove impediments, which has symbolic weight and meaning. Study your life for a few weeks after you spend a solid hour shifting your layout to accommodate movement. Note any correlations, even subtle ones, between what you do to your home and what happens in your life.

In a room that needs to serve many functions at once, be mindful of the balance between ease of movement and style. Keep pathways clear and make sure that any items that can be used in different areas of the space (like the chic stool pictured here) are easy to relocate.

Exiting Complaint Mode

Practicing a solution-oriented mindset at home takes work, but getting good at it has untold benefits. In the beginning, you want to create a series of small wins to activate more of this capacity for yourself. Once small wins are achieved, you generate the momentum to tackle bigger challenges.

Return to that list of "not enoughs" you made on page 80 and reflect on how long these complaints have been active in your home. Many of us are more comfortable staying in complaint mode than we realize. An effective way to untangle complaint loops with a partner or family members is to list the home-related disagreements you consistently have. What have you tried to do together to solve the problem? List the top three things you've done to actively address this and assess what worked and what didn't. Inhabit a solution-oriented mindset and reflect on whether there are any creative solutions you haven't thought of.

One former client constantly fought with her husband about his tendency to leave tools for half-finished decorating projects in the living room for weeks. Indeed, she had a point. Tape measures, paintbrushes, and tape were piled up on a beautiful desk that was the focal point of the room. His excuse was that he worked on the projects every few days and there was no other place to corral his tools. I saw his desire for ease in completing projects and understood his motivation. Yet they were both stuck in a recurring loop of annoyance, which kept them from seeing the solution in front of them. Sitting in their foyer was an empty chest that we moved into the living room to serve as an end table. The space inside it was more than enough for the project pile. This small win shifted a dynamic. They just needed to take a step back.

We all have our blind spots, holding on to limiting belief systems through no fault of our own. These patterns are not created by conscious choices, but we can consciously choose to break them. Where in your life are you standing in your blind spot? Addressing these issues may seem impossible, but the good news is that you can easily decide to be open and curious, to learn the answers, little by little, with new intuitive information. Through this awareness, you come to realize not only that you are ready for something new but also that you are capable of receiving it. You don't need to maintain the status quo, even though you may believe that there's no other way. Have compassion for yourself.

Here's another piece of good news: Your brain rewards you when you plug into a solution mindset.

BLIND SPOTS

Some patterns are inherently harder to see than others. Impossible, even. These are our blind spots, which live in our unconscious until we choose to make them conscious—or someone else points them out to us. The people closest to you see right into your blind spots, the same way you see right into theirs. You'll know someone is hitting on one of your blind spots when you get defensive and reactive. You may find yourself arguing for the status quo in tolerating a messy home, for example, rather than finding a solution for it. And you're right—there is always a good reason why a situation is as it is. But the key to shifting the situation comes in deciding you want to shed light on your blind spots and try to fix them. You need to lay down your defenses and own them. This can be painful, but removing the blinders is the most efficient way to upgrade your life. Left unchecked, your blind spots develop into tripping hazards (see page 88) that you will have to address eventually. If you're not being solution-oriented in your home, chances are you are not being solution-oriented in other parts of your life.

Dissolving vs. Decluttering

In my experience, dissolving is way more potent than decluttering. The latter doesn't really work, at least not for long. That's because if you fail to examine *why* you hold on to things or arrange your home as you do, you aren't getting to the root of the problem. In fact, you are apt to adopt the same pattern all over again. In contrast, the dissolving (*solve*) process that is central to Spatial Alchemy not only helps clear space but also helps you understand why you let things pile up in the first place. You are uncovering and separating out layers of identity, personal values, and belief systems rather than simply purging without introspection or insight.

So, just as the ancient alchemists dissolved lead in order to understand its composition before refining it into gold, you can use alchemy to break down the layers of your current space.

Start with visual clutter. This includes broken items, piles on the floor, things you haven't thought about or engaged with for years, and the like. Addressing this obvious layer first affects your body immediately, because clutter is calcified energy in physical form. Often, it exists beyond where you can see it and in neglected corners. Dissolving clutter alleviates the effects of overwhelm when your life is chaotic.

At the outset, I suggest scheduling at least an hour or two every couple of months to keep this layer in check. Remind yourself that you will never achieve perfection, and that holding that as a benchmark for yourself may cause more harm than good.

From there, the dissolving process gets less obvious, more nuanced. The second layer is tied to outdated identities. Some personal items maintain a strong hold on you because they are tied to meaningful periods of your life—your childhood, maybe, or singledom. To explore the second layer, consider anything that you've had for a while and ask yourself whether you would acquire it again today. (We did a similar exercise in Part One—on page 65—when calling forth the Future Self.) I have a table, for example, that I designed years ago for an event I was styling. It has moved with me a few times since. Today, it makes no sense to keep it in my family space, and yet I am attached to it because it represents an identity I am nostalgic about. *If I were to let it go,* I tell myself, *I'd be losing a part of me that is dear to my heart.* However, it's not serving the present-day me—or my Future Self. This is what I mean when I refer to the death of an old identity. Facing the finality of that can resemble a form of grief. We tend to protect ourselves from painful feelings, but in this *solve* exercise, the more painful the action, the more powerful it is. Rather than equating the act of letting go with the death of something, celebrate the space you are clearing to make way for an emerging identity.

As you navigate this process, more insights about identity will emerge. For many years, I had a collection of castoffs I'd found on the street. Each had been refurbished and had a "trash-to-treasure" story to go along with it. (In my experience, many people who live in New York City hold a special fondness for, even a perverse pride in, street finds.) Although I had fun upcycling these items, in my current home they reinforced an outdated mindset. I put my energy into living as a "starving artist" in my twenties and thirties, in my version of *La Bohème* in Brooklyn. *I can't have a creative life if I am wealthy*, I told myself, so I eschewed home objects that felt even vaguely fancy. My unconscious belief was that money would somehow taint my creativity. Once I dug into the layers of my collection of castoffs, I realized I didn't have to live out that bohemian fantasy in my everyday surroundings. And as I shed that identity at home, I became more comfortable expressing my deeper desire for abundance. I realized that creativity didn't need to be defined by a limited stereotype. I could aspire to be creative *and* financially successful. The two needn't be mutually exclusive.

Layer three in the dissolving process includes objects with sentimental value: heirlooms, hand-me-downs, and gifts, all of which can be especially difficult to part with. We project emotional energy onto them, and believe that we'll be betraying someone dear if we get rid of their stuff. *This sofa that was in my grandmother's house represents her love for me. If I were to give it away,* you tell yourself, *I'd be letting go of that love and of my grandmother.* But in reality, that love exists outside of the sofa, not within it. Dissolving means assessing if each piece is in alignment with your Future Self. If you never figured out how to make the item work in your home, the heirloom

is more of a burden than an asset. Consider gifting it to someone who could make better use of it. Reframe the act as passing on or bestowing the object, sharing the good energy with someone new rather than discarding it.

The final layer to address is tied to your beliefs around wastefulness. Make a list of the things in your home that you truly love. What percentage of your practical items (storage pieces, dish towels, dustpans and brooms, sponges) elicit a *hell, yes!* response over a *meh* one? If many of them fall into the latter bucket, what else in your life are you putting up with? Where are you settling, instead of surrounding yourself with things, people, and experiences that are more in line with your true pleasures? You may buy inexpensive things at the big-box store without putting much thought or energy into them, but they can reinforce an entrenched thought pattern that you are trying to dissolve. Instead, replace those objects with things you select for their aesthetic as well as practical value.

Keep in mind that not all belief systems are negative. As you dig through the layers of your belongings, you will start to uncover positive signs, which helps reinforce the kind of energy you want to plant. Maybe something in your home was acquired to represent reaching a milestone in your life or achieving success in your career. Pieces like this signal *I am worthy* to your brain. Accentuate them by putting them within framing devices, like just beyond a doorway, so they're the first things you see when you walk through.

Instant Gratification

You know the yummy feeling you get immediately after restyling an area in your home? There's a science to it that involves dopamine and your brain's pleasure centers, and you can use it to help motivate you to disrupt a constant complaint loop. I found this helpful in combatting my beliefs around time scarcity (see page 84). By breaking my time down into manageable chunks, I was finally able to make changes in my home that I'd been putting off for years.

The trick is to make restyling stints short, so they feel achievable and not overwhelming. You want to circumvent the "I don't know where to begin" brain freeze and get straight to an "I've got this" attitude. I've developed my own brain hack for this, which starts with scheduling a thirty- to forty-five-minute session on my calendar once a week. I set a timer, tune out all other distractions like my phone, then get to work restyling one shelf in a bookcase, or the coffee table, or the foyer console, or the bathroom countertop. By keeping the project doable—anything I can complete in that limited time without feeling rushed—I'm able to see it through.

The reward is always a serious dopamine hit. We all get a shot of this "feel-good hormone" when we finish something we've avoided. Instant gratification is a serious confidence boost, and when this exercise is over, I always notice the following:

- The fresh energy of change is a mood enhancer that lasts for days.

- I have a sense of pride that I got myself to move past my resistance and "lack of time" excuses.

- The beauty of the work gives me aesthetic pleasure. This is a great momentum builder.

When I need a small win, restyling my kitchen counter and shelves always does the trick. Objects with sculptural shapes—think shapely pitchers, pedestal bowls, and curvaceous cutting boards—are particularly useful in distracting the eye from clunky countertop appliances.

We all have items that take away from rather than add to our self-worth, yet our attachment to them endures. I struggle to get rid of rickety lamps, uncomfortable chairs, slightly broken sculptures, and the like, but every time I do, I appreciate the release of stagnation that follows.

DECODE YOUR STUFF

Every item you've chosen to live with has a narrative that is linked to a feeling. Track which items in your home don't make you feel good, and most likely they'll be linked to identity layers you are ready to part with. What are the biggest pain points for you? Here are some of mine:

– Things that never quite worked in my home

– Things that feel emblematic of an old version of myself

– Things that don't function properly

– Things I forgot all about

– Things that don't communicate the sense of abundance I want to feel

– Things I would not buy again, if given the choice

When I want to cling to these things, out of nostalgia or fear of change, I ask myself whether I value that item more than I value the emerging identity I want to create. I set my pace based on my comfort level, and sometimes I release things even when it feels uncomfortable in the moment. A week or so later, I realize how much of a burden that item was and acknowledge how much space opened up for me once I let it go.

Sitting with the Emptiness

After dissolving and shedding layers of stuff, take time to celebrate the space you've opened up without rushing to fill the void. There's wisdom to be uncovered in doing nothing. Some spiritual practices advise adherents to sit with the emptiness of these liminal spaces and to breathe into them. As you embark on the *solve* part of this process, difficult feelings may arise. After all, we cling to our belongings because they form part of our identity: who we are and, importantly, who we were. The advice to sit still is similar to the wisdom of not jumping into a new romantic relationship right as you come out of an old one. You need to spend time on your own, lest the same patterns be repeated with a different person. What you're looking to do here is change the underlying programs. To expand into the after, not revisit the before.

Practice the high art of listening deeply to your space and your intuition. Allow yourself to access the wisdom of the void. Ask yourself how these changes feel—in both good ways and bad. How do they affect your sense of self? What is emerging? What will become possible in your life once you let go of those identity layers?

When you live with fewer things, there is more clarity, less mental noise. You can hear your space speaking to you. It begins to tell you what it wants. Many interior designers prefer to approach a new project when the space is empty, so they can start by listening to it. The more you clear, the more you will hear. But it doesn't happen all at once. Have patience. New ideas and wider perspectives reside in the void and come into consciousness both quickly *and* gradually.

The rewards for that waiting are clearer purpose, direction, and the ability to see next steps. "Stillness, silence, and solitude are required for developing a life," says transformational guide Jamila Reddy. "You have to be able to hear yourself and feel yourself. How else can you know what you want outside of the noise of what other people want for you?"

Remember, don't rush to fill the void. Practice listening deeply, and let the space remain empty for a period of time, creating an intentional vacuum until you can start to feel what it wants to fill it.

The hardworking kitchen is often the fullest space in the house. Try dialing down the clutter by even 20 percent. The newfound spaciousness should give you a surprising sense of clarity.

PART THREE

SMALL MOVES, BIG SHIFTS

Bringing intention into reality begins with a series of small steps.

You've cleared your home of what is no longer serving you, spent time sitting with the emptiness, and tuned in to the silence. Now it's time to build things back—not as they were, but in alignment with the emerging identities you want to cultivate. You want to reinforce the energy of the Future Self until it feels tangible and unbreakable. The best way to do that, without crashing and burning or regressing? By starting small.

In the following pages, you'll begin to understand how a succession of small moves leads to bigger, more quantifiable results. After all, *coagula* is a multilayered process, just like the step of dissolving (they are two sides of the same coin). As you begin to recompose the layers of your home to reconstruct your life, you are transforming your intentions from a fluid, energetic state to a solid physical one. The home is the best place to begin to master this concept; it is your personal petri dish.

The objective is to seed the identity you want to grow, by way of mindful upgrades and deliberate pattern creation, or coding, throughout your home. What distinguishes this approach from other home design and maintenance practices is that the process is not defined by "before and afters." Your home is a constant work in progress, a spiral rather than a linear progression, as is your life. Meaningful change is ongoing, never fixed. This awareness is what makes the process distinct.

Choose one special thing you've already identified (on page 52) to represent your Future Self. This is the first strand of the web you are weaving. And just like when a spider spins its own web, the shape will not appear for a while. The first few strands may even look random. Guided by the pages that follow, you'll make more small, achievable shifts to keep you moving in the same direction. You don't have to know every single future step all at once. Somewhere around the sixth shift (or strand), the new form will begin to take shape. This is where you begin to feel the momentum, which will at some point take on a life of its own.

On the following pages, you will learn:

- How to upgrade your daily routines to create powerful shifts in your life

- How to harness the symbolism of the objects and textiles you surround yourself with to reinforce your emergent identity

- How to transfer the energy you want to seed into physical form

- How to establish new patterns by coding your home, in small ways, to invite the experiences you want more of into your life

- How to program a confidence boost into your life by way of your home's focal points

Elevate the Everyday

Daily tasks are alchemical gold, precisely because they are mundane, a word with roots in the Latin term for "world" (*mundus*). These everyday actions are more worldly than spiritual. Over time, they become rote. We don't even think about doing them or assign value to them. But what if we chose instead to elevate these small but necessary routines of our daily lives? How could infusing small chores with grace and care impact our life experience?

Start to pay attention to everything that you do on repeat, those movements that have become second nature to your body: brushing your teeth, having your morning coffee or smoothie, making the bed, exercising, taking a shower, preparing meals, getting ready for bed, reading a book, and turning off the light.

Take notice of where those movements can be upgraded to be more pleasurable. What are the items associated with each task: toothbrushes, mugs and water glasses, cookware, linens, and bedside reading lamps? What cup do you drink from every day? How does it feel in your hand? Does it please your eye? Do you look forward to holding it? Do you keep it in view or tucked away?

Consider where any part of your daily routine seems strained or inefficient. Do you tell yourself that you'd like to change it when you have more time, money, energy? Look for small tweaks you can make to upgrade those routines. This is how we begin to channel the Future Self into the quotidian experience.

Review your notes as you begin to envision a few manageable wins. What is the easiest shift? For me, it's the cup I drink from all day long. Try finding one that represents the energy you want to bring into your life. Set an intention to solidify that energy into form (this is the essence of *coagula*). What cup would represent the energy you want to drink in? Select a few options and note their differences, and consider how energy and physical appearance relate. Aesthetics are important, but so is the feel of the cup, its presence.

Imagine that with each sip you take, you are physically consuming the energy you desire. Spread that feeling to other everyday objects, like a pen, an alarm clock, a watering can, a set of cloth napkins, a saltcellar—anything you will use frequently. Start feeling the *expansion* energy. Stoke it and keep feeding the energy that pulls the Future Self toward you.

Each cup embodies an energy based on its form, material, and color. If you want to feel more fierce and grounded, drink from a sturdy clay cup like the red one (far right). If it's levity you're after, a quirky glass cup (far left) will help get you there. A Japanese-inspired minimalist cup (top) can help calm an overscheduled routine. A cut-crystal cup with a gold handle (bottom) invites in old-world luxury, which signifies dignity.

Symbols &
the Subconscious Mind

Symbols are the gateways to our subliminal minds. Big brands know this. Think of the power of the Target symbol and how it grabs your attention, for example. We can do the same for ourselves, in our homes.

Dreams communicate with you in the language of symbols; you can communicate back to them in the same language. Tune in to your dreams and any associations, images, and symbols that appear in them. In the waking dream called life, choose symbols that hold power for you, stacking them in intentional combinations to create sequences of meaning, which then message a deeper, nonverbal part of your brain. The language of symbolism is that simple.

The sun, for example, has been featured as a symbol in various cultures over thousands of years (the Ancient Egyptians, the Mayans, France under Louis XIV, modern Japan, to name just a few). Why? Because the sun gives life and grows everything it touches. It's no wonder, then, that people and cultures have long wanted to associate themselves with this life-giving energy, and so they embraced the power of this universal symbol.

Stealing a page from their book, I decided to use a sunburst mirror as my video conference background when I was starting a new business. At first, I cringed every time I had a meeting with that background behind me, with a halo of rays coming out of my head, as if I were a medieval icon. It didn't feel like me. I was skeptical that it would even have a measurable effect, but the year I hung that mirror behind me was an extraordinary period of growth for my budding business.

My goal was to build a full-time career out of Spatial Alchemy rather than continuing to accept styling gigs that didn't feed my spirit. Working toward that with symbols was a stretch for me, but I'm always open to experimenting on myself before suggesting practices to others. In the time that the sun symbol was hanging over my head (about fourteen months), I realized my dream, which required me to trust in myself completely. I was able to earn the same income in that first year of focusing on Spatial Alchemy as I had in the previous year in the well-trodden role I was trying to move away from.

Was it only the sun symbol that shifted the game for me? Of course not. On their own, each of the small moves I made would have had an almost imperceptible effect. But by making a series of intentional choices, I was crafting an environment that reflected the Future Self energy I wanted to feed.

Because symbols are inherently archetypal, you are often able to feel them intuitively. The main block that most people experience is a lack of understanding of the symbolic meaning of imagery. They are more attuned to the beauty or value of art than to the way it affects their psyche.

I did a symbol reading for a friend who was devastated after her divorce. Right by the entrance to her home, she had a lithograph of a goat by a famous artist, her most prized piece of art. Yet this goat, with a tag on its ear, looked dejected, as if it knew it was going to be slaughtered.

This piece had been hanging in her home for so long that she had stopped seeing it, focusing more on the value of the art than on the effect it was having on her subconscious. Once she could objectively see the sadness of the piece, she decided she no longer wanted to feel this way. After selling the piece, she used the money to buy another piece of art, one that held the energy she desired to merge with. This new choice of imagery in her home helped to create the mood she wanted to experience and made way for the version of herself she wanted to step into.

My advice is simple: Know yourself. A piece of incredible but angsty art is most likely not going to have a negative effect if you're already feeling grounded, stable, and evenly regulated. However, if you are going through a fragile period, you may want to consider the placement of artwork that is at all challenging, or put something around it that can balance and soften the energy.

The view from the desk in my former office. The radiant sunburst mirror was centered between images of the sky (an air element) and trees (earth elements). These symbols, taken together, formed a dialogue of rootedness, connection to spirit, and outward expansion that aligned my spirit with the career aspirations I was working toward, keeping me engaged and motivated.

Decoding Common Symbols

The world of signs and symbols is so vast, there are countless books devoted to it. Here, I include just a few commonly used examples so that you may begin to understand how these work with your unconscious mind. With practice, you can become adept at seeing how the symbols you've chosen to live with affect you. Are they conveying the messages you would consciously choose for yourself? Beyond these four categories, you may start to identify others and learn to program your art and objects more deliberately.

Humans

The emotional states represented by any images or sculptures of humans in your home have a direct influence on your psyche. Whether those representations consist of family photographs or surrealist paintings, it's important to discern the emotions you have chosen to surround yourself with, piece by piece. Imagine the humans depicted in your artwork living with you (in effect, they already are). Would they add to your life or detract from it? Pay attention in particular to old photographs of yourself and the narrative you associate with that time in your life. Does it still feel relevant to have those pictures hanging on your wall?

Animals

Animals are associated with specific characteristics. If you choose to incorporate an image of a particular animal in your home, make sure that animal's traits are in line with the purpose of the space. For example, a leopard-print chair has big-cat energy, symbolizing fierceness. It is also activating, so it's a good choice for an office. In a bathroom, not so much. Tortoiseshell or symbols of land turtles hold a slow and solid energy. Faux tortoiseshell boxes would help settle the nervous system when the goal is to unwind, sleep, or slow down.

Nature

In alchemy, water is associated with the emotional realm (see page 30). Look around your home to see if any water images you have are calm or stormy. Fire symbols such as lightning, sunrises, or deserts have transformative and purifying effects. The symbol of air, such as views from high places, reinforces perspective and clarity. Plant patterns, including images of trees and botanical prints, represent earth energy, encouraging growth and fecundity.

Transportation

Symbols of transportation (including cars, ships, trains, planes, rockets, and boats) work on two levels. The first level represents travel, whether it's a journey to a new destination or a long, tedious commute. When you have symbols of transportation on your walls, ask yourself where the journey of your life feels like an adventure and where it feels like a slog. How do the transportation symbols on your walls align with the kind of movement you desire? The second level of symbolism is that of speed. Whether the pace of your life feels too slow or too fast, you can choose modes of transportation on your walls to reinforce the tempo you want to experience.

SEE YOUR SYMBOLS

Chances are your home is already awash in symbols. Are you aware of what they are saying to you? Examining them in the present moment helps illuminate them and encourages further experimentation.

1. To begin, stand in front of each figurative image in your home in turn. What do you think of when you look at it? What cultural and personal associations do you have? (If the image provokes no association, note that, too.)

2. Now let's zero in on the symbols you view from your bed in the morning. The first thing you see when you awaken programs your subconscious brain. Sit on the edge of your bed and scan your objects and the images that hang on the walls. What narrative lies beneath each object in your view? If they could talk, what would they say? How do these objects and narratives relate to one another?

3. If you haven't moved the symbols you see every day around in a while, do it now. Approach the activity with an awareness of the subtleties of each symbol. Sense what happens in your body when you've finished repositioning things, and track it in the days and weeks ahead.

Parachutes symbolize the courage to take big leaps and trust that you will land smoothly. I hung this enormous artwork featuring a bright yellow parachute as a reminder to rely on my trust "muscle" when I'm feeling anxious about the future, rather than ruminating.

What you see at the end of a long hall is impactful, because you walk toward it many times a day. One potent image (like the ancient column pictured here) does more to reinforce resolve and determination than a bunch of smaller pieces would.

USE FOCAL POINTS
WITH PRECISION

Focal points are all about directing attention in order to program specific messages into the body. Many spiritual teachers follow some version of the saying "Where attention goes, energy flows." By placing power objects in key focal points, you are making the most of this dynamic, focusing your attention in a specific spot in order to bring about your desired outcome.

To understand the potential of focal points, start with doorways. They frame and highlight the significance of whatever you see through them. In addition, the act of crossing a threshold and entering a room activates your attention. What you see when you stand in a threshold space subconsciously programs your brain. Consider the messages you want to program your brain with. They should reflect the specific energy you want to reinforce in your life. For example, if you want to bring more abundance into your life, work with both the physical and the symbolic (see page 108) elements of growth and expansion.

1. Close your eyes and picture all the frames and thresholds in your home. What do you see through each one? What emotion does that evoke? Is it the emotion you want to be feeling?

2. Now, mentally scan the rooms in your home, looking for objects with the energy you want to seed.

3. Try relocating anything you identified, moving it in and out of view from threshold spaces and clocking your reactions.

4. If nothing in your home comes to mind or works the way you want it to, consider bringing in something new to frame from a threshold.

POTENT FOCAL POINTS

Consider any and all of the following perspectives within your home when deciding where to position a focal point.

1. From your bed: the first thing you see when you wake up in the morning and the last thing you see before you fall asleep at night.

2. From the entryway: what you see when you walk through the door.

3. Reflected in the bathroom mirror: what's behind you when you're brushing your teeth or engaging in other self-care rituals.

4. On central surfaces: what's placed on a mantel or coffee table in the living room, on the sideboard in the dining room, or on bookshelves.

5. From your desk: what you see when you are not looking at your computer screen.

6. Over the sofa: where your eye lands when you look into the living room.

To make a focal point even more effective, surround it with symmetrical pairs of like objects. Every balanced layer you build in amplifies the energy of the central piece. Here, that includes the identical shelves hung high on the wall, the tiger prints, and the elegant chairs that flank the sideboard.

Generating Momentum

When you take the individual objects you chose (see page 107) and begin to create tableaux around them, you are solidifying energy into more complex arrangements, to reinforce an emerging identity layer through coding.

How does coding work in the context of the home? With technology, coding means designing instructions that make it possible for a device to do what you want it to. The process works similarly within our physical environments, by way of new energetic templates (via your stuff) you set up to upgrade your mindset and expand your self-worth.

Let the specific word you are coding for guide you. (Refer to the list you made on page 65 if you need a reminder. My word was *dignity*, something I am continually coding for.) You are looking to create surroundings that embody that word. Repetition is important, so place your code in more than one room, and specifically at eye level, for reinforcement.

Coding your home with the energy of dignity will create more prosperity in your life. This is because dignity is the antidote to (or the opposite frequency of) the energy of victimhood. The more dignity you code throughout your home, the more you reinforce your state of "already having." This is what pulls manifestation in the prosperity direction. (More on coding your home for dignity, as well as other desirable states, on the pages that follow.)

The initial coding is a series of small moves in a call-and-response process. It's important that after each shift, you stand back and observe the process at work. This is not a one-and-done activity. What you are looking for are subtle correlations between what you do to your home and what transpires in your life.

You want to keep the momentum going as you introduce these shifts, to continually propel yourself forward. At some point in the experiment, a small but positive event will occur in your life that you will know, in your bones, is related to the shifts in your home. Take note of it. The more you practice noticing the magic, the more magic you will begin to notice.

To me, the classical shapes, long necks, elegant handles, and burnished tones of these Byzantine-inspired pieces carry the code for dignity. By spreading them throughout my home, I plant an invisible but powerful grid that will propagate this energy across the space and into my life.

CODING FOR DIGNITY

To expand your sense of self-worth, begin to uplevel
your daily routines until you feel a noticeable impact on
your psyche. This can also affect how you carry yourself
physically, which may at first even make you uncomfortable,
as if you're faking. Keep going. When you ease into the
feeling of more dignity in your body, continue putting
objects in place that elicit that energy. Maybe it's a flush of
warm energy in the chest or belly as you silently note a sense
of pride every time you pass by your handiwork.

THREE WAYS TO CODE YOUR HOME FOR DIGNITY

1. Restyle your desktop. I regularly pick up each item on
   my desk and hold it in my hand. I want to make sure the
   things feel more upscale than ordinary. When necessary,
   I add a new special something, like a pencil holder or a
   monogrammed desk blotter, to reinforce my career goals
   and aspirations.

2. Release all the old, mismatched dry-cleaner hangers and
   random one-offs in favor of a new matching set. Nothing
   makes a closet look dignified more quickly. I use only
   two kinds of hangers in my closet: velvet-covered ones for
   fabrics that slip off easily, and wooden ones for heavier
   coats and jackets.

3. Decant dishwashing liquid, mouthwash, and other
   unattractively packaged household necessities into
   elegant glass bottles. The prettier the bottle, the more
   you upgrade your daily chores.

Want to send your psyche a powerful message of self-love? Design your bathroom with dignity. Here, because the toilet is the focal point, a pair of elegant sconces flanking the entrance to the room and the gold-framed art and a plush rug within it all add a sense of grace to this utilitarian space.

I channeled my inner child when styling this blanket chest turned bar area. The diamond rainbows in the artwork, kooky French-horn lamp, tilted vase, and squiggly wallpaper (which purposefully clashes with the other patterns around it) were chosen to encourage optimism and inner buoyancy.

CODING FOR LEVITY

Just as laughter is the best medicine, levity is the best antidote for feeling weighed down. This type of coding is useful when you feel overburdened, negative, or pessimistic. Bringing humor and delight into your home helps turn those feelings around. You want to inject a good dose of fun into the process of shopping for these things and arranging them.

FOUR WAYS TO CODE YOUR HOME FOR LEVITY

1. Buy something that you find funny, even if it's a little out there. The point is to take a risk and stretch beyond your norm. Let your inner child make a design choice. I once bought a lamp fashioned from a French horn (opposite) that made me smile every time I looked at it.

2. Choose a boldly patterned bedspread to wake up a quiet bedroom. You can fold it away when you sleep so that your rest isn't affected. I love a vintage bedcover in a flame-stitch pattern or superwide stripes and large-scale florals for this.

3. Hang panels of fabric on your walls for a hit of strong, bold color without taking the time to paint. I go to a fabric store and buy a strip long enough to go from the ceiling to the floor, then secure it with brass tacks.

4. Try fun things when hanging art, like putting an outrageously big piece of inexpensive art on a bathroom wall or something whimsical across from the toilet, at eye level.

CODING FOR CLARITY

When you are having trouble making a big life decision—and this indecision can often last for years, painfully—try coding mental clarity into your home. First, created a dedicated zone, which may be a bookshelf or a whole room, depending on how much clarity you're looking for. Next, do several rounds of *solve* (see page 94) in that zone, as clarity frequently results from removing what is unnecessary from your life. Lean in to minimalism, at least for a short time, then follow the tips below.

FOUR WAYS TO CODE YOUR HOME FOR CLARITY

1. Replace decorative objects that have complex or random shapes with simple geometric ones such as obelisks, triangular sculptures, or classically shaped vases.

2. Materials that are transparent (like colored glass, Lucite, or resin) reinforce the essence of clarity. Consider putting clear objects on a surface in front of a window to make the most of the light shining through them.

3. Reflective surfaces (think mirrors) double everything in front of them. Make sure what you see in them isn't disordered.

4. Assess your lighting situation in the evening to see if there are any dark corners that could be illuminated. If so, choose a lamp with a simple graphic silhouette.

The value of negative space is often overlooked, but it is essential when your goal is to code for clarity. The simple, graphic lines of the objects in this under-the-stairs area foster clearheadedness, while ample room around each piece creates a silhouette of its own.

Layer upon layer of bright, bold patterns give this room a transportive effect that immediately activates the body. Crisp, modern stripes and graphic polka dots offset the abundance of traditional ikat, floral, and block prints that surround them.

Pattern Play

Patterns are rife with symbols, and they energize any interior space. And because patterns repeat, they are especially potent. Think of a room upholstered in all solid fabrics and then one with plenty of figurative pattern. The contrast between the two is palpable. I often begin the design of a room with a pattern to inform the experience I am trying to create. You want patterns to be in line with your own desired experience, to help you move in that direction. As you introduce more pattern, consider the following:

- Big patterns make impactful gestures. To create a bolder experience, increase the size of the pattern. One large pattern can even serve as its own focal point. Marrying bold color with a big pattern is especially activating; you may need to temper that commanding presence with some minimalism if you're looking to create cohesion.

- For florals, the smaller the pattern, the sweeter the effect. Small-scale florals often impart gentleness. Large-scale florals, on the other hand, can feel lush and luxurious.

- Repetition creates structure. The more you layer different patterns together in one room, the richer it will feel.

- Pattern can be soothing. To mix patterns softly without leaving the "calm" range, limit the color palette. Imagine patterns in a range of sizes in "neutral," for example.

- Mixing periods makes a statement. Putting modern patterns on traditional furniture shows gutsiness. The same goes for pairing traditional patterns with modern furnishings.

- Think outside the material. Patterns are not limited to the obvious elements, like fabrics and wall coverings. The way you arrange your bookshelves creates a pattern, with colors and textures forming shapes and sequences. When you see the books on the shelves as blocks of a pattern, the effect is more intentional, less random.

Recognizing When Shifts Have Started

In most cases, merging with a new identity is a gradual progression, sometimes taking years. Slowly you begin to see yourself differently, by nature of marinating in a certain environment. Spatial Alchemy is about catalyzing and refining this process so that it feels less bumpy and more supportive.

After several rounds of *solve et coagula*, and as you gradually become adept at using your home to deliberately reprogram your psyche, you will begin to notice a sensation similar to a computer operating-system upgrade. Your life feels like it's running better. In place of bugginess there is a consistent, subtle smoothness. You may even sense a quickening, thanks to the momentum you are slowly building. Examples of the types of cues you may feel, signaling that you are moving in the right direction, include:

- Slight shifts in your mental state: feeling lighter and brighter
- Bodily responses such as goose bumps occurring more frequently
- Greater curiosity and excitement on a regular basis
- Feelings of pride
- Insights that are beyond your usual perspective
- Subtle signs and synchronicities that gradually become more clear (like getting a message from someone you've been thinking about or having your lucky number appear several times in a row)

What all of these signs point to is a correlation between the small moves you have been making and the changes you are experiencing. It doesn't matter whether these are especially impactful on your

The tipping point occurs when you become aware that your behavior, self-perception, and self-worth are being affected.

life at the moment; in fact, it's better to start small and learn to track the cause and effect. This is how you learn to gauge your ability to manifest. The tipping point occurs when you become aware that your behavior, self-perception, and self-worth are being affected. This is where the identity merge becomes more obvious. Be prepared for others to comment on it. People may say things like "You look different. What have you been up to?" That's when you know your inner shifts have taken hold. When your confidence and self-assurance expand, people notice your radiance, sometimes before you do.

If you are still lacking the confidence to make big design decisions, it helps to know that you don't have to. Build the readiness with small steps that become greater than the sum of their parts. The more confident you feel that you can execute a design plan from the perspective of the Future Self, the

more significant your next moves will be. This includes making any big purchases for your home. Give yourself a long leash if you're feeling up to it, and see where it takes you. Be sure to read all the way through the section on the emotional realm (beginning on page 134) before you invest in any major upgrades. Keep a steady pace and work your way up to any big decisions like which sofa to buy.

Maybe you don't feel that the process has begun to take effect. Remind yourself that this stage is rooted in living with the small, seemingly insignificant shifts rather than recognizing results right away. Staying the course when the shifts are not yet tangible is a big-time alchemical superpower, one that every practitioner must learn at some point. The key is to be patient. Make a conscious choice to trust in it—and in yourself.

PART FOUR

DESIGNING FOR EMOTIONAL BALANCE

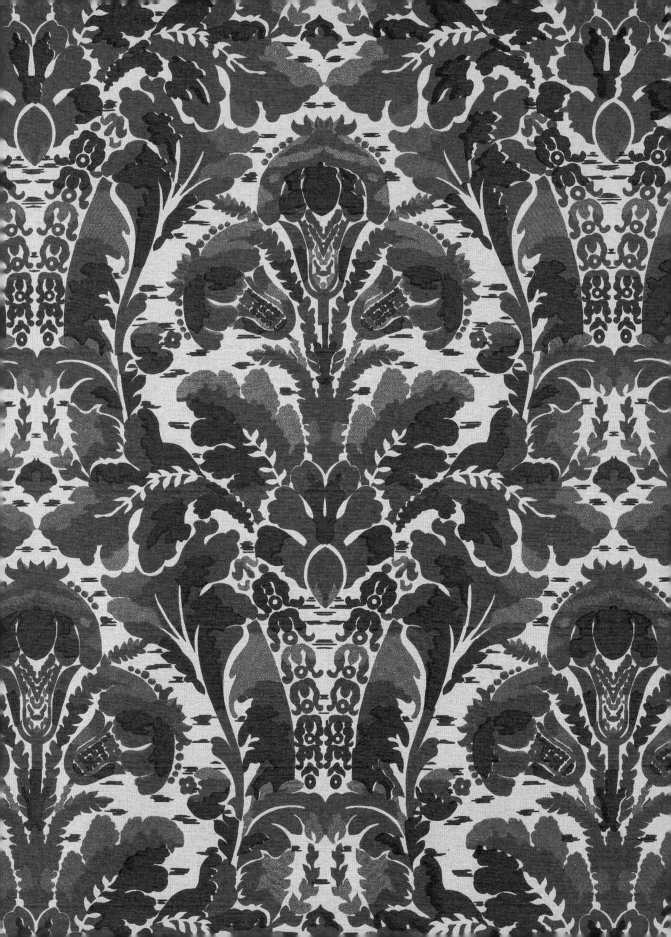

The home is the ultimate emotional support system.

At this point in your exploration of Spatial Alchemy, you recognize that your home is a catalyst for change. Like an ancient alchemist, you consider its potential for refinement. Now, we'll focus on the various ways you can rely on your home to help you achieve emotional regulation. The capacity to respond gracefully to our emotions, rather than trying to control them, lies within each of us. Whether we feel sad or anxious or mad, we can learn to meet those feelings, in positive, proactive ways, with our homes serving as powerful, steadfast allies. In turn, we can ride our waves of emotion, even in the face of overwhelm, rather than looking for ways to escape them.

Emotional regulation starts with recognizing your habitual response patterns, many of which are deeply ingrained, as they developed in childhood. Taking note of situations in which you find yourself stuck in a loop familiarizes you with your own snags. Every time you are stressed or in a funk, do you lash out at those around you or reach for an unhealthy crutch that provides temporary relief? As an antidote, reflect on your needs in those moments and think about how to set up your home as a support system before you start to spiral.

In the pages that follow, we will cover the three pairs (or dyads) of emotional opposites—stability and fluidity, activity and passivity, and connection and privacy—that are the core building blocks of any home. If you are suffering from burnout, for example, after being mired in activity mode for weeks on end without taking a break, you can right yourself by leaning in to the energy of passivity. To anticipate this need (and head off any potential imbalance), design your home to be ready for it. Start by placing a comfy chair in a quiet spot, and maybe work your way up to installing a cushioned bench beneath a window. The point is, we all need a place to curl up and take shelter from a torrent of feelings, so that we can more easily and responsibly pick ourselves back up again. This back-and-forth process of designing for emotional needs facilitates down-regulation throughout the home.

In giving ourselves the home-as-safe-space experience, we create deeply nourishing havens that increase our odds of experiencing an overall state of comfort, balance, and fulfillment. Along the way, we become more emotionally available to ourselves.

On the following pages, you will learn:

- How to identify the six core emotional energies that underpin a supportive home and use design choices to reinforce them

- How to assess the level of each energy within your space and bring them into balance

- How to create rooms that are at once highly functional and wholly supportive of your emotional needs

- How to identify where opportunities exist to build emotional support into your home to provide greater levels of self-acceptance and care

The Six Core Emotional Energies

Working with design clients at all stages of life, I've learned to recognize six core emotional energies that form the building blocks of any home: stability, fluidity, activity, passivity, connection, and privacy. The six energies are organized into three dyads, or pairs of opposites, and are at once specific and universal, micro and macro. Together, they form the center of the Spatial Alchemy approach. Once you are aware of these six core energies, you can begin to balance them throughout your home to create harmony. By making space for each of them, we can call on that energy with more assurance thereafter. If your life feels out of whack in the outside world, you can begin to use your interior world to course-correct.

When a home is put together with the right proportions of the six energies, it is coherent, beautiful, functional, and whole, and that greatly impacts your emotional state. The "right" proportions vary by individual. Only *you* can determine what feels right in the present moment. The balance will naturally need to be adjusted and calibrated throughout your life, in response to changing experiences, goals, and circumstances. As self-awareness emerges, your home responds in kind. The result is an active feedback loop that supports your emotional needs.

Stability & Fluidity

Balancing rootedness with flexibility keeps you from becoming calcified or chaotic. We have all been in homes with too much stability. They feel heavy and boring, with an emphasis on imposing furniture, squares, and straight lines. The overall impression is one of rigidity, lifelessness, perfection, or stagnancy. Conversely, a home with an excess of fluidity seems anything but safe and secure. The ground feels shaky thanks to the scattered and unfocused energy. People who live in overly fluid spaces often complain of lack of consistency both in their homes and in their lives.

The goal here is balancing desire with security: *How do I feel rooted and secure while also expressing my authentic self in my home (and life)?* Navigating this dialogue is a foundational life skill, and designing it into your home will enhance your capacity to maneuver it in your life.

Activity & Passivity

This is the spectrum of movement and respite. You want to design some spaces that generate growth and others that soothe the system as it lies fallow. Staying active is viewed as a positive, and yet many of us override signals from our bodies when it's time to take a break. We keep working and producing, failing to see signs of burnout. Creating areas of passivity in the home allows the body to regenerate effectively, especially if you are someone who continually takes on too much, to the point of exhaustion. You may need space to breathe more deeply, unplug, and unwind to recharge and reset. Lean too hard toward passivity, however, and you risk falling into a rut. In fact, an excess of passivity can encourage depression, procrastination, or inertia. Connecting to what inspires you and planting that active "fire" energy in your home creates a spark that feeds your motivation.

Connection & Privacy

This dyad is concerned with the negotiation between self and others. Knowing how to regulate it allows you to manage boundaries, welcome connections, and maintain healthy relationships throughout your life. An overemphasis on connection leads to self-neglect, while too much privacy can result in social isolation. A balance allows for steady companionship and solitude in equal measure, for awareness of all members of a household, and respect for personal space. When a home encourages both energies simultaneously, its inhabitants can be alone together, quite happily.

READ YOUR HOME'S EMOTIONAL BALANCE

Before you begin implementing changes in your home, you need to zero in on existing conditions inside yourself. What do you long for more of in your life? What kind of emotional support can you give yourself to address that longing? Our goal in this exercise is to design that emotional support into your home.

1. Having read about the dyads on the previous page, ask yourself how they relate to your longing. Where is the biggest imbalance in your life?

2. Now, let's see how this relates to your home. Stand in the middle of each room—the living room is a good place to start. Keep your eyes open and slowly do a 360-degree turn. Where is this life imbalance manifested in your home?

3. Think of three words that describe the feelings you currently experience in each room, including uncomfortable ones. Putting feelings into words validates them. The key lies in being honest with yourself. If you are feeling neutral, you are not digging deep enough.

4. Now we'll find opportunities to change that balance. To feel more rooted, safe, and supported in your life, turn to Stability (page 143). To align with more flow and creativity, turn to Fluidity (page 155). To encourage more motivation and empowerment in your life, turn to Activity (page 169). To encourage more restoration, softness, and slowness in your life, turn to Passivity (page 183). To sense more belonging and intimacy in your relationships, turn to Connection (page 195). To lean in to the intuitive mind in order to align with your spirit and soul, turn to Privacy, page 211.

5. Now tune in to the energy that is the exact opposite of one of the words you chose. (If you were focused on the feeling of chaos in step 3, for example, now dial in to calm.) Feel that and breathe it in. This is the antidote energy you want to use in this room (and likely, throughout your home).

I lived in this apartment for ten years without realizing how completely out of balance it was. It had an abundance of activity and fluidity (even the wallpaper was on the move) but no space for the passivity and stability I desperately needed.

Spatial Alchemy & the Chakra System

The core emotional energies of Spatial Alchemy correlate to the chakra system first cited in the Vedas, the oldest known Indian text. Just as the chakras illustrate the harmonious flow of energy throughout your body, from the bottom (root) to the top (crown), Spatial Alchemy aims to create a harmonious flow of energy through your home.

1. The root chakra is located at the base of the spine and represents earth, the root of all things. In Spatial Alchemy, stability allows you to feel more grounded in your home and in your life.

2. The sacral chakra relates to creativity and sexuality and is associated with water. In Spatial Alchemy, fluidity entails moving with the flow of energy and translating your desires into the physical world of your home.

3. The solar plexus chakra is associated with fiery energy located in the belly and gut, your body's powerhouse. In Spatial Alchemy, activity represents expansion.

4. The heart chakra is associated with air, due to the relationship between the heart and the breath. Considered love energy, this chakra represents the capacity for kindness, compassion, and empathy for yourself and others. In Spatial Alchemy, passivity means self-care, integration, and regeneration of the body through the home.

5. The throat chakra is associated with communication and speech, as well as honesty. In Spatial Alchemy, connection is used to create and strengthen bonds between yourself and others.

6. The third eye chakra is linked to intuition and inner wisdom. It is connected to light and seen as a pathway to enlightenment. In Spatial Alchemy, privacy bridges your body and spirit, allowing for the deliberate cultivation of intuitive knowing and trust.

7. The crown chakra is the center of unity and collective consciousness, and is regarded as the gateway to the cosmos. This crown is a portal out of the physical world and into the nonphysical one. It is not under the aegis of our home.

CROWN CHAKRA
◆

THIRD EYE CHAKRA
◆

THROAT CHAKRA
◆

HEART CHAKRA
◆

SOLAR PLEXUS CHAKRA
◆

SACRAL CHAKRA
◆

ROOT CHAKRA
◆

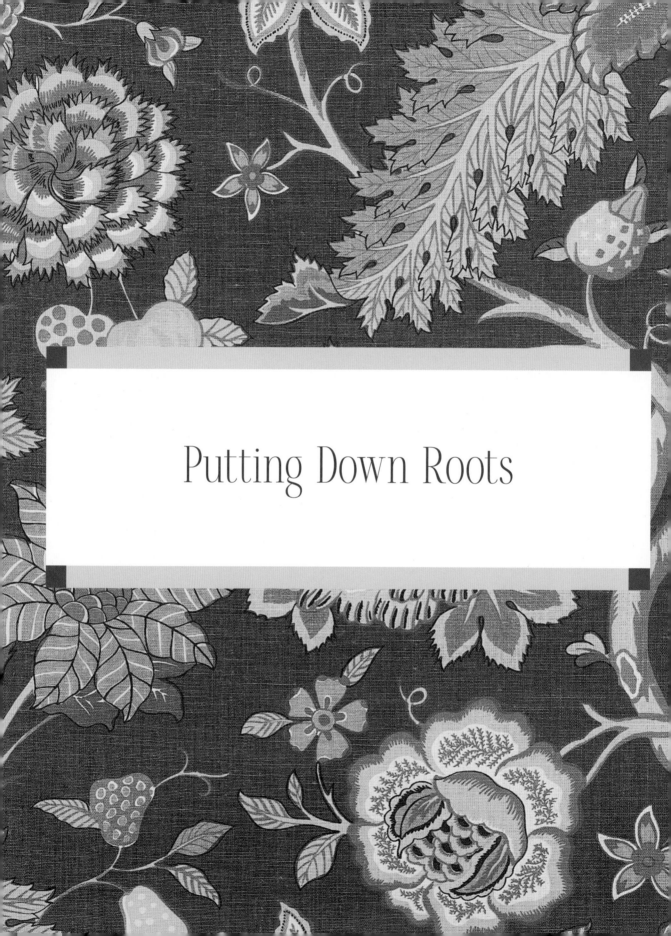

Putting Down Roots

DESIGNING FOR

Stability

When your home feels stable, your psyche is held in place, like a tree is anchored by its roots. This fosters self-confidence and self-esteem. You can more easily regulate your emotions when you sense that it's okay to stay put, to relax and sink into this base.

In my twenties, I judged stability as dull. I didn't appreciate the value of rootedness, choosing instead to live within a creative whirlwind that bordered on chaos. I thought this would make for a free-spirited, exciting life. As I grew older, however, I realized that my nervous system craved constancy, so I started inviting it in. I began a nonverbal dialogue with my home, buying one large piece of art to replace a gallery wall, swapping out bright colors for grounding ones, lowering my bed closer to the floor. My body began to tune in to a new bandwidth. Once I was able to balance those opposites— the chaos and the calm—I learned to accept stability and even embrace it.

One way to reinforce the energy of stability in your home is to add substantial elements at major milestones in your life. If you enter into a committed relationship, for example, buy a sturdy piece of furniture that honors that pact. When you land a promotion or a new career opportunity arises, choose something weighty to commemorate your achievement. Investing in these foundational pieces centers the body in the midst of change and allows it to expand into the upgrade.

The need for stability in one form or another is constant, however—not just in times of change. To settle into a space that lacks a solid foundation, start with anchor pieces that define the room. Think high-quality, solid, built-to-last investment furnishings with a palpable presence.

Keep in mind that the amount of money you spend to acquire an item is not as important as the level of intention, care, and commitment you bring to it (as is true of any worthwhile partnership). The point is not to literally invest a lot financially, but to bring a level of deliberation to your decisions.

KEY WORDS

Rootedness
Security
Consistency

Investment
Commitment
Symmetry

KEY FURNISHINGS

- A substantial dining table with solid legs
- A sofa with presence, that you can sink into
- A bed with a statement headboard and a frame that sits low to the floor
- Heavy chests of drawers and armoires
- A thick-topped desk with sturdy legs
- A freestanding bathtub (I prefer claw-foot tubs for their weight and profile)
- Rugs large enough to sit under all the furnishings in a room

Fig. 1 *Thick-legged wooden tables broadcast stability; here, an overscale basket underneath acts as an additional anchor.* **Fig. 2** *This low-to-the-floor bed and solid wardrobe lend gravitas to an otherwise airy, soft bedroom.* **Fig. 3** *Notice how the traditional side tables and lamps and heirloom rug help ground the many eclectic elements of this space.* **Fig. 4** *Flanking a curved chest with a pair of matching chairs and symmetrical art telegraphs balance and consistency.*

This dining room features all the hallmarks of stability: dark wood paneling with rectilinear molding, a thick-legged table, artwork in repeating square shapes, and traditional botanical wallpaper. The arrangement is balanced by the transparency of the woven chairs and the curved handles of the vase.

KEY DETAILS

- Light fixtures at floor and ceiling levels for a sense of containment
- Wood paneling and other types of molding
- A pair of dressers in the bedroom
- Two candlesticks on the mantel
- Even numbers of artworks hung in a grid
- Antiques and heirlooms, such as a set of family china or vintage crystal—anything that feels substantial and has a provenance
- Woods with a deep, visible grain
- Accessories made of metal and stone
- Ceramic tiles
- Terra-cotta urns, ideally planted with potted trees
- Weighty fabrics like leather and suede
- A color palette of deep, saturated tones
- Botanical patterns in wall coverings, textiles, and artwork

A STUDY IN STABILITY

GETTING
SETTLED

MICHELE AND STEPHEN, TWO WRITERS living in upstate New York, didn't feel secure in the house they shared with their young children and dogs, even ten years after moving in. Overwhelmed by making design decisions, Michele was stuck in default mode. She opted for cheap, generic furniture so she wouldn't have to worry if the kids or the dogs trashed it. As a result, she had no connection to her home or anything in it. The house lacked a dominant style or unifying voice. A few of the rooms sat completely dormant. The couple wanted a home that looked smart and sophisticated but also felt comfortable and unassuming.

We started in the sunroom, building on the energy of its ample sunlight. After clearing out the nondescript furniture, we brought in a vintage bamboo desk and surrounded it with potted trees to suggest a solarium. The abundance of natural elements was intentionally chosen so that the family would feel as if they were finally putting down roots. We hired a local artist to paint a beautiful mural in orange tones to complement the existing terra-cotta floor tiles. To contrast the brightness of this new "summer" living room, we painted their adjoining "winter" living room a deep purple-brown to accentuate the low ceilings, the wraparound built-in bookshelves, and the large fireplace mantel. We leaned in to the cottage feeling inherent in the proportions of the room and turned it from cold and bland to sultry and cozy.

Next, we tackled a tiny TV room where Michele had crammed a massive sectional. Rather than getting rid of a bad decision (by tossing the sofa), I played into it by installing a dark vintage rug (no more worrying about stains) and hanging densely patterned William Morris wallpaper (a nod to the English style the couple loves). I made the wallpaper "louder" than the sofa, which diminished it. The new room feels intentionally scaled up and timeless, as if it's been that way forever. A combination of bold moves (the dark rug and wallpaper); weighty, solid pieces (the sectional sofa); and strong color choices creates both active energy and grounding stability—just what this couple needed to commit to their home, finally, and to welcome in the sense of security they were longing for.

149

Stability &
the Entryway

How many times have you rushed into your home, left your shoes on, and dumped the stuff you were carrying in random places without stopping? If your answer is "Too many times to count," it's time to take a good look at your entry setup.

Creating an entryway geared toward slowing down and recalibrating your body puts stabilizing energy into action, as it honors the transition from the outside world to the safe inner sanctum of the home. Cultures all around the globe mindfully mark this transition. It is common practice to take a moment to pause, sit, remove your shoes, take a breath, and recognize that you have just crossed your own threshold. This is an excellent example of setting up your home to reinforce the energy of groundedness.

As children, we learn how to transition from the exterior to the interior world. Nursery school teachers build in ample time in the morning to train children to make this switch smoothly. Natalie Cohen, a psychoanalyst and former nursery school teacher, believes that the key to making these "holding spaces" work is establishing structure and paradigms that encourage containment yet still leave room for freedom of movement and energy. This translates to a system of boxes, bins, cubbies, and hooks—a place for everything, and everything in its place.

So how do you create the most stabilizing threshold experience in your home? With a space that facilitates retraining your body to settle in place and activating a feeling of calm, centered security from the moment you step in the door. Place a beautiful, comfortable chair where you can immediately sit and take off your shoes. With this small gesture, you are programming your mind to accept that you deserve a comfortable place to pause. Deservedness becomes integral to your daily experience.

In my home, replacing a slick, super-hip console with a chest of drawers in the foyer illustrated simple yet profound need fulfillment. I was so used to the console accumulating clutter that I stopped noticing. I had to constantly search for a place to set down my gear when I walked in, and to try to locate things I needed when I walked out the door, like bug spray and market bags. The search rattled me every time. Introducing drawers felt like a gift after years of living with the impractical console. The foyer now felt much more grounding and stabilizing.

When we walk into an entry space that suits our needs, our bodies get the message that it's okay to stay put. It lets us know that our home is a space where we are held and supported. We can be our authentic selves. This is the essence of stability.

While most of the decorative elements in this foyer are white, their large-scale, sturdy shapes keep the space from feeling flighty. The console table is covered by a table skirt that hides practical plywood shelves beneath.

QUESTIONS
FOR THE ENTRWAY

Think of every move your body
makes with the same level
of TLC a nursery school teacher
shows their students as they
learn the steps of arriving
and leaving. Consider the
choreography of your body as
soon as you walk through
the door:

- Where do I put my coat?

- Where do I put my bag?

- Where do I take off my shoes?

- Where do I put the mail and
  any packages?

- Where do I put the things
  I'll need when I leave again,
  like keys?

FOUNDATIONAL
FURNISHINGS

- A chest of drawers, for storing
  market bags, dog leashes,
  stamps, sunscreen, hats and
  gloves, and more. Alternatives
  for small spaces include hooks,
  baskets, floating shelves with
  drawers, ledges, and stacking
  boxes.

- A chair, bench, or stool, so you
  sit and take a moment upon
  arrival or departure

- A mirror, to see yourself on
  the way in and out, and for
  guests to do the same

VISUAL CONSIDERATIONS

- Mind the focal points (page 118) and symbols (page 108). Whatever energy you want to activate in your life should be represented by the items you first see when you cross the threshold.

- A nice lamp, ideally one that you need to switch on and off manually. That simple action is a way of intentionally "turning on" and marking the transition in a routine that can become a ritual.

- An eye-catching tray or trays for loose change, keys, and other small items you empty from your pockets upon returning home

OPTIONAL ADDITIONS

- A rug to further stabilize and ground you in the space

- A chandelier or other weighty pendant lamp to connect the floor and ceiling

- Elements of self-expression that represent who you are to yourself

Flowing with Change

DESIGNING FOR

Fluidity

When I want to build my capacity for resilience, I turn to the energy of fluidity. While stability represents the trunk and root system of the tree, fluidity serves as its branches. A home designed for fluidity allows your body and psyche to adapt and adjust, just as branches work their way around obstacles as they grow. You program into your home self-expression and creativity to move with challenges, rather than suffer through them. More than any of the other energies, fluidity also allows for creative expression, which staves off some of the heaviness that comes from an abundance of stability. With my background in styling, I appreciate the joy that comes from arranging and regularly rearranging various elements in my home.

Consider adding elements of fluidity when your life is riddled with moving parts and you're asking more of your home than it can handle. Maybe you've just welcomed a new baby or married into a blended family with members of varying ages, needs, and schedules. You might be juggling multiple demands—work, family, and other commitments—and consistently feel like you just can't keep up. Emotionally, you're constricted by all this irregularity, unable to express your desires while scrambling to get stuff done. Anything you truly want for yourself gets put on the back burner as the daily balancing act overtakes the pleasures of life. Things quickly become dull, and you feel frustrated when you can't break out of that rut.

While helping to accommodate these and other fluctuations, fluidity also serves as the antidote to the rigid or controlling elements of stability. Bridging these two opposites means establishing a symbiotic system in your space. Start by introducing a few hardworking furniture items and accessories that can respond to a host of needs. Multipurpose pieces—expandable dining tables with extra leaves; storage systems that corral gear of all kinds behind doors—calm what can feel like an excess of uncertainty. Establishing order through multitasking furniture programs your body to feel lighter. When you bring order to the disorder, your body gets the message: *I've got this. My systems are in place. Bring it on.* Your home is prepared to go with the inevitable flow right alongside you, as an ally, with ease and ingenuity.

155

KEY WORDS

Responsiveness
Resilience
Experimentation

Multitasking
Creativity
Self-expression

KEY FURNISHINGS

- Modular furniture, for maximum flexibility
- Accessory pieces on wheels (bar carts, media centers, side tables)
- Upholstered folding screens, especially as room dividers
- Storage benches that double as seating
- Murphy beds
- Swivel chairs
- Fold-down desks

Fig. 1 Bar carts glide easily from room to room and can be transformed into food service trolleys at a moment's notice. **Fig. 2** Long-armed swing lamps and an open shelving unit create a variety of lighting and storage options in a loft-like room. **Fig. 3** Gallery-style arrangements of artwork allow boundless opportunities for self-expression and embody the essence of flow. **Fig. 4** A borderline stodgy, giant round pedestal table in the foyer becomes responsive and chic when covered in layers of colorful textiles that hide the shoes stored underneath it.

By placing a simple modern table in a corner of the living room, you expand your options for functionality, giving yourself a sometime desk, sometime bar, sometime library corner, sometime game table. The curved-back chair with an animal-print seat cushion adds movement and whimsy.

KEY DETAILS

- Adjustable and layered lighting (a combination of high-wattage bulbs on dimmers, pendants, tabletop lights, floor lamps with movable arms, and candles)
- Amorphous and wavy shapes
- Off-kilter items like three-legged tables and chairs
- Armchairs and other upholstered pieces with pronounced curves
- Asymmetrical arrangements of accessories, like three candlesticks on the mantel
- Trendy colors and surfaces to balance investment pieces
- Transparent surfaces (such as Lucite resin) that let the light through as it moves over the course of the day
- Quirky and unusual small pieces like stools and umbrella stands
- Decorative outliers, as in one or two things that feel out of character for you or aren't represented elsewhere in your home

SPACE SHIFTERS

Folding Screens

IF I HAD TO NAME ONE FURNISHING that most embodies
the energy of fluidity, it would be the folding screen. I
firmly believe that every home should include at least
one. I see them not only as infinitely practical room
dividers but as pieces of art. You can use folding screens
to soften corners, which is particularly useful in a large
living room when you want to establish "rooms within
rooms." I often introduce one to create an extra seating
area off to the side of a sofa. All you need to add is a
chair, a lamp, and a side table and you've turned an
empty corner into an opportunity. Folding screens are
also invaluable when you want to cordon off an area for
games or hobbies, for much-needed privacy, or to conceal
a storage space.

Visually, when you divide a room into three planes
(more on that on page 264), a folding screen brings the
eye up into the second third of the room, which instantly
helps with layering. The screen's folds make it sculptural,
adding dynamic energy to even the most minimal
environments. And, of course, the fact that you can
upholster a screen with fabric, paint it, or add an element
of texture to it means it's versatile and malleable. In other
words, the embodiment of easeful adaptability.

*A folding screen (pictured at right) helps hide unsightly electronic
equipment and blocks glare from a window when you don't want to
hang curtains. Here, the bold pattern of the screen's fabric also
adds architectural interest to the room.*

160

A MORE
ARTFUL
ARRANGEMENT

LAUREN AND DOUGLAS ARE A PAIR OF CREATIVE EXECUTIVES living in a two-bedroom Manhattan condo with fantastic light, river views, and an enviable collection of art. Yet for all its assets, their home wasn't working. They needed the apartment to serve multiple purposes at once, with a better sense of rhythm, easeful flow, and more room for their creative pursuits.

Their decor and their life circumstances—a toddler and two busy careers that often called for long hours of working from home—were at odds. Fluidity was the energy they needed, given the family-career-life shift that was forever in flux. They needed workspaces and places to connect as a family, to entertain family and friends, to hang out, to express themselves, and to strengthen their partnership.

Yet everyone—and everything—was top of each other. No privacy, and less couple-time connection than they desired. While watching movies together, they sat on separate pieces in the living room. In the primary bedroom, a clunky desk discouraged both intimacy and rest. Throughout the apartment, their mish-mash of furniture didn't fit the space, support their routines, address their needs, or reflect their style.

The goal was clear: to create adaptive spaces within the existing rooms to accommodate full-time work and plenty of off-hours downtime. We began by prioritizing workspaces for each of them, as far apart as the apartment allowed. We designated an area where the couple could reconnect after their toddler's bedtime, set up a drawing space for Douglas, and found a spot for Lauren's large keyboard.

A table with extensions increased their options for dining. Now the space feels casual and intimate for dinners for three, yet easily expands to accommodate gatherings of six or more.

To make the living room meet their needs, we upended the layout and reoriented the furniture. A game table in one corner created space for the couple to catch up at the end of the long workday. Importantly, it's away from their office spaces and the family table, providing an "every night is date night" spot.

Artwork also serves as a bridge between connection and privacy. We arranged a grid of thirty framed pieces of Douglas's art along the corridor that leads to their bedroom. Not only did it strengthen their bond, but it also reinforced his desire to paint more and inspired Lauren every time she went from their bedroom to the main living areas.

Though seemingly small, each shift produced considerable impact. The apartment now provides more pleasure to everyone within it, not only because it looks better but also because it functions so well and meets the needs of the three people who live there.

Fluidity & the Dining Room

Picture your most easygoing, adaptable friends, the ones who take nearly everything in stride. These people don't balk at last-minute dinner guests or panic when plans change or schedules shift at the last minute. They embody the energy of flex spaces.

Even if you don't fit that description, you can learn to program more unflappable, "anything goes" attitude in yourself using your home. Flexibility is a skill set that can be practiced and honed until it echoes through every aspect of your life. It starts with bringing awareness to your needs and desires, then developing a step-by-step strategy to meet them. Most of us have more needs and desires than we do rooms. How do we pack them all in without bursting at the seams? Look to barely or rarely used spaces that are ripe for reinvention. Start by giving yourself permission to use rooms other than the way they were intended.

The dining room is an excellent example. In many homes, it serves as a spillover space, for better or worse. How often do you find yourself scrambling to clear off the dining table because you have people coming over and it's piled high with mail, kids' belongings, and wayward household items? In my own dining room, we were devoting precious storage space to fancy plates that we rarely used, at the expense of the things that we frequently needed like craft supplies. We reworked our systems, trading a traditional sideboard for an armoire that makes crafting sessions much more manageable. Now there's no need to quickly shove things out of sight when we want to eat at the table. Maybe your dining room doesn't even really need a table! Using the room as your yoga/fitness studio instead might allow you to adopt a wellness regimen more readily.

Ultimately, dining rooms and other flex spaces are about the dialogue between your needs and your home. Flexibility lies in how much ease you have in this dialogue, and your ability to respond to your current needs with tenderness and wisdom. Invariably, your needs will change over time, so make a plan to reassess flex spaces every six months or so.

If you rarely entertain, a small dining table offers more flexibility for other pursuits, and space for additional furniture. This modern pedestal table is easy to move; the large glass-fronted cabinet increases storage possibilities.

QUESTIONS FOR THE DINING ROOM

Consider how your home can accommodate shifting desires as you move through it over the course of the day and the seasons of the year. Make a list of needs to address as you contemplate the answers to the following questions:

- Are there any desires I keep ignoring? What do I need to fulfill them?
- What do I do when I want to exercise at home?
- How do I make space to work at home or for kids to do homework?
- Is there a good space to designate for crafting projects and hobbies?
- What do I do when unexpected guests drop by?
- Do I have everything on hand for overnight visitors?

FOUNDATIONAL FURNISHINGS

- Multi-leaf dining tables; consider round tables that break up square rooms with a different shape and accentuate connective energy
- Large storage pieces rather than bitsy ones, to disrupt the cycle of chaos and project a seamless sense of order
- Skirted console tables with shelves, for plenty of concealed storage
- Upholstered dining chairs, which not only provide more comfort but can also be slipcovered and re-covered when you want to shift the look of the space

VISUAL CONSIDERATIONS

- Artwork that does double duty (e.g., hung on a bookshelf to cover storage boxes behind it)
- Sculptural occasional tables, cool stools, and small side chairs that can be easily moved from room to room to change the vibe
- Rotating gallery walls of personal photos and mementos
- Floating open shelves, which add visual appeal as they divide spaces
- Quirky table lamps on consoles for when you want an alternate lighting option that's less formal than a chandelier

OPTIONAL ADDITIONS

- Woven baskets with lids
- Brightly colored or metal trays to break up monotonous surfaces and to use for serving guests
- Vases, sculptures, and large bowls. I add or subtract a few new pieces every so often to keep things fresh and buy small items that are borderline ugly or not my usual taste to shake things up.
- A rotating array of seasonal flowers and branches

Fired Up and Ready to Grow

DESIGNING FOR

Activity

Of the six energies of Spatial Alchemy, activity is most aligned with the trajectory of the Future Self. Think of how you feel on January 1, after you've expressed (if only to yourself) how you hope to change in the New Year. Maybe your plan is to get healthier, or launch a business, or finally break free from a dead-end relationship. You have the internal spark and the optimism that goes along with achieving that goal.

When I need support to help me stick to an especially challenging resolution, I call in the energy of activity. The seductive quality of this fiery force goes beyond the mental realm. It activates the body to *do* something—not just anything—deliberately and with focus.

Active energy propels and strengthens resolve. To invite it into your life, start by infusing it into your home decor. Active spaces teach your body to build momentum and expansion, to express your agency in an assertive way. Any room—not only the home office or kitchen or similar "workspaces" but also pass-through areas and retreats like dens and sunrooms—can benefit from the powerful energy that drives motivation.

Look to bold elements to cultivate meaningful growth, anything that aligns with the intensity and stimulation you need to get unstuck. Shifts in scale are also critical to active energy, as they are instant attention-grabbers. Consider oversize framed artwork that gives you a jolt every time you see it, for example. Or an investment piece placed in a prominent spot, to remind you of past success and keep that energy in focus. Have you ever considered that diplomas in executive offices aren't just there to impress visitors? They also reinforce the graduate's sense of accomplishment where they may need it most, at their place of business. It's self-worth made manifest. Find something that works the same way for you, and set it in a prominent spot where you will see it every day. The objective is to generate and sustain steady progression.

Prominent placement, strong contrasting colors, and repetition are all guiding principles in active spaces. Opt for arresting furnishings and art. You want the inherent energy of each piece to continue to motivate you. The best active elements propel you toward your goal and keep your intention front and center.

KEY WORDS

Motivation
Resolve
Inspiration

Courage
Boldness
Expansion

KEY FURNISHINGS

- Oversize (conspicuously out of scale), bold furniture pieces and accessories
- Statement lighting, like giant floor lamps or pendant lights
- Artwork that commands attention
- Waist-high stands or pedestals to hold large sculptures, vases, or plants
- Painted furniture with presence

Fig. 1 Strategic splashes of bright yellow in the kitchen can kick-start resolutions like cooking and eating healthier foods. **Fig. 2** Sweeping marbleized wallpaper and graphic floor tile transform a ho-hum rental bathroom into a statement of confidence. **Fig. 3** Dynamically patterned, colorful storage pieces draw the eye, spark motivation, and complement boldly shaped accessories. **Fig. 4** Overscale paper lanterns are a classic, low-cost way to make a big statement in a space, and a hit of bright red—always, anywhere—harnesses fire energy.

In this highly activating space, black walls and a neutral rug accentuate, by contrast, the range of bright hues in the framed artwork, side table, and linens. When shapes are kept simple, color and pattern become the main event, without having to compete for attention.

KEY DETAILS

- Houseplants (caring for them feeds your consciousness as it encourages your own growth)

- Radiant pieces that symbolize expansion, like sunburst mirrors and tall candelabras

- Geometric patterns (on wallpaper, textiles, upholstered pieces, floor coverings)

- Strong, bold (even clashing) colors (saturated reds, oranges, bright yellows and greens)

- Reflective surfaces that bounce light around—lacquered items, mirrors, high-gloss and high-shine elements

- Small (or large) touches of gold or other precious metals—on bowls, pots, and frames—to symbolize financial success

- Materials juxtaposed in one piece, like a metal and glass accessory, for active tension

- Wallpaper in unexpected places, like on the ceiling or the back of shelving

SHIFTING
GEARS

KARA, A STUDENT OF MY ONLINE COURSE, had long hoped to transition from her full-time corporate job to a business of her own. This career shift transpired over several years, in a big open area off her dining room that she had claimed as an office. The space reflected her one-foot-in (a strong desire to leave corporate life) and one-foot-out (still clinging to her past identity, out of fear of diminished income) headspace. Because Kara's office was cluttered and neglected, it left her less confident about making the career leap and kept her in a self-perpetuating cycle.

How could she help herself break out of this state of professional limbo? First, I zeroed in on her need for more active energy in her office. The most obvious source of stagnant energy was her desk, which she'd bought from a clearance sale fifteen years earlier. She couldn't see how it was keeping her from stepping into the emerging identity she wanted to cultivate. She was struggling to build a new business on top of an outdated identity.

Imagining her Future Self in the new business she was envisioning, she gravitated toward a more elegant persona as its embodiment. Finding a desk that was both feminine and solid took some searching, but when it was in place, the energy immediately shifted.

Next, we focused on her office storage, which consisted of three bookshelves of varying sizes and materials, holding random books and papers. This is when it became clear how little she was focusing on her business. She got (literally) active and released things that belonged to her outdated identity. To house what remained, she chose one large, solid bookshelf that made a statement. The space now provides the external motivation to spark her internal motivation.

As Kara frequently takes videoconference meetings for work, we created a backdrop that was bold but would not overshadow her, with a grounding paint color that looked good with her skin tone. Curating her backdrop to make her look strong on camera boosted her confidence to get her business off the ground.

She also replaced her old office chair, which was ergonomic but didn't feel sumptuous. Since she spent more time there than anywhere else, she chose a cushy vintage chair and upholstered it in a bold print. To create a focal point while she sat in the chair, we curated a fluid "altar to her future business," changing the objects (and images in the gallery wall above it) with the seasons and her moods. An antique pair of lamps provides some visual stability.

With all of these energizing components in place, the home office is finally working for—instead of against—Kara.

Activity &
the Home Office

The home office is the essence of active energy, promoting our capacity for growth and expansion. Its purpose is simple: to make room for you to focus and function optimally. A well-designed workspace lets your body know that you are supporting your goals and that necessary tasks are a pleasure, not a grind.

How do you design a space for forward movement? The key is to create an environment that's almost (but not quite) too good for you. It should feel like a stretch, as if you are tethering yourself to the future, more bountiful self, rather than to present-day you.

Many of us have experienced how it feels to sit in bland, unmotivating cubicles in office buildings or in classrooms without interesting colors or textures, day after day. Our brains shut down. Work becomes drudgery. In putting together a home office, we get to design the space to align with the way we want work to feel: challenging, exciting, evolving, fulfilling. On pages 72–73, I went into detail about how I made a series of bold decorating decisions that anchored me to my own career intentions as I looked to expand my design coaching business.

Even without a room to designate as a home office, you can set up a space that encourages productivity. Be sure to choose one spot, however, and resist the urge to work wherever you happen to find yourself. If you are constantly in flux, roaming from room to room, moving forward takes more work. You are not attaching to your goals.

Focus on what the placement of your chair and work surface will mean for the position of your body. How does it feel in relation to the room? You want to find your "command position." Strong, powerful CEOs generally sit facing the door, or diagonally across from it, with a solid wall behind them. In feng shui, facing the door is believed to allow you to see opportunities. Conversely, having your back to the door keeps you on alert, in fight-or-flight mode, which is not ideal for focus. For obvious reasons, looking directly into a corner impedes growth.

After trying the command position out on myself and hearing feedback from my clients, I've found that this arrangement works every time; my body feels like it owns the space.

Adding a large, bold monochrome rug to a neutral office changes the entire mood of the space. Here, the bright yellow door telegraphs optimism and amplifies motivation.

COMMAND CENTRAL

The way that you deliberately design your home office directly impacts your career success. Beyond material choices of furnishings, floor and window coverings, wall colors, and textures, pay close attention to how your body is held in place. Consider three zones within the workspace based on your command position:

1. The area behind you. Your backdrop serves two purposes: to give you support, and to frame you for meetings (especially for videoconference calls). The ideal is a solid wall, in a color that flatters your skin tone. If that's not possible, position your desk parallel to the door to the room. Look at the symbols that appear behind you carefully; they are nonverbal communication. Do they reflect the energy you want to animate in your life?

2. Your "power wall." Not what is behind you, but what you see while you are seated. This is what you are stepping into, your calling, the North Star of the Future Self. It should be equal parts inspiration and motivation. A mood/vision board, a collection of framed awards or other symbols of personal accomplishment or achievement, or a single piece of artwork— anything that's highly personal to you and actively energetic.

3. What is surrounding your body and what you are touching while working. Namely, your desk and chair. Go for quality, well-made pieces that feel sturdy and substantial. They represent how you view yourself. Do they inspire your body to experience purpose and advancement? Avoid castoffs, basic corporate office chairs, or seats borrowed from the dining or living room. You likely spend as much time here as you do in your bed. Why not teach your body it can have it all?

In my previous home office, I needed to balance the active elements with others that kept me centered and focused. Paperwork was collected on trays behind me, atop a pair of fabric-draped filing cabinets holding essential office supplies, allowing me to maintain a minimal, clutter-free desk— and a clear head.

QUESTIONS FOR THE HOME OFFICE

Take time to think about your home office setup and whether it is supporting your work and career goals. Consider how it is (or is not) allowing you to complete tasks efficiently and, ultimately, to grow and stretch professionally as you answer the following questions:

- How do I want to be seen by the world?

- What items express what I want my career to feel like?

- What would help me feel even more supported in this space?

- What do I see in front of me and how can it be easily enhanced?

FOUNDATIONAL FURNISHINGS

- A desk that resembles the success you're aiming for: solid, functional, stable, with drawers to contain clutter (unless you're a true minimalist)

- A chic, luxe-feeling chair that holds your back securely

- A shapely statement lamp to break up the boxiness of the desk

- A storage piece large enough to hold unsightly office stuff. You want to minimize visual noise, which inhibits focus and growth.

VISUAL CONSIDERATIONS

- Substantial bookshelves behind the desk to add a sense of solidity

- A large-scale piece of art for impact, as long as it's not chaotic. Avoid gallery walls, which can be distracting; you want to be the center of attention.

- A mood board: Gather a collection of treasured and inspirational visual items that resonate with the Future Self. Place it in front of you to keep you motivated, and update it regularly. If your board hasn't changed in more than six months, it's a relic.

OPTIONAL ADDITIONS

- A cord management system. Nothing telegraphs disorder and confusion like a wayward bundle of cords. I use little fabric tubes (my local dry cleaner sews them for me) that I call cord condoms. One condom fits all the cords, and the plug can be in a basket on the floor.

- An office altar. Mine consists of symbolic objects that I want to strengthen my career resolve—a $100 bill, a mini Buddha, and a candle.

- A second chair or another place to sit. Choose comfortable seating, where you can take a break, read something non–work related, and check in with your Future Self.

Resting to Replenish

Passivity

When I start to sense that my system is overrun, it's time to call on the energy of retreat and recovery. Passivity works to regulate my nervous system by decreasing the number of stimuli in my surroundings. It also balances the intensity of activity with tenderness, allowing me to give over and be honest with myself.

The relationship between this energy and emotionally aware secure attachment (see page 28) is strong. Close your eyes and remember how you felt pampered when you were a child, by crawling under the covers, or slipping into a warm bath, or curling up in a soft chair. This is the energy you want to re-create as you respond to emotions that knock you sideways, whether you're grieving a loss, nursing an injury, recovering from a breakup, or suffering from burnout.

Passivity is all about the body. When you inhabit spaces set up for this energy, they let you know that it's safe to rest, that you are allowed to be soft and gentle and to receive comfort from the outside in. They give your body permission to be unproductive, to sit or lie still for a spell. Then, when you're ready, you can return to the growth cycle with renewed energy and determination.

Bedrooms are the most obvious passive spaces, but look for other places throughout your home—anywhere that allows for burrowing. When you feel depleted but are not yet ready for bed, is there a specific spot where you can retreat without surrendering to sleep? Passive spaces teach your body to honor the distinction between respite and sleep as you get centered, unwind, and seek balance. I like to put a "pause spot" in every room. Creating resting spaces involves bringing awareness to what soothes you and building a dialogue with your nervous system and its down-regulation mechanism.

In my home, I designated a daybed for passivity. It's deliberately placed where the sun hits at midafternoon, so I try to spend a few moments there.

For those who prefer upright time-outs, an armchair with an ottoman is a better choice. Give your body a variety of ways to rest, indoors and out. Consider hammocks and chaise lounges and a range of upholstered pieces.

Finally, keep in mind that passive spaces don't have to remain that way forever. You can use this energy temporarily, or in small areas of larger rooms. The more of your senses you can address, the more potent the experience of passivity you create for yourself.

KEY WORDS

Nourishment
Soothing
Comfort

Receptivity
Healing
Replenishment

KEY FURNISHINGS

- Daybeds and cushioned benches
- Armchairs with soft upholstered arms that you can sink into
- Upholstered headboards that allow you to lean back and be softly held
- Wall treatments that soften your walls, like textured wallpaper or hanging textiles
- Rugs with a pronounced pile, for softness underfoot

Fig. 1

Fig. 2

Fig. 3

Fig. 4

Fig. 1 *Dark, tone-on-tone sitting rooms create a womb-like atmosphere that's tranquil and restorative.* **Fig. 2** *Outfitting a hard bench in the foyer with a thick, tactile sheepskin softens the transition from the outside world.* **Fig. 3** *The fuzzy wool on the back and seat of this leather club chair provides additional comfort, and a nice variance of textures.* **Fig. 4** *To heighten passive energy, play with a limited but mixed range of soft, feel-good fabrics. This bedroom's textiles include linen, cotton, and luxe velvets in the sheets, pillows, coverlet, and headboard.*

Bathrooms are prime replenishment zones. (Why else are they called "restrooms"?) The more your life feels lightning fast, the more you want to immerse yourself in a deep soaking tub and linger there. Here, a vintage rug, a curved table, and a chair with fabric panels soften the inherently hard surfaces of bathroom materials.

KEY DETAILS

- Window coverings that block out or diffuse light
- Tactile textures (to invite touch)
- Felted baskets and bins
- Attractive speakers for listening to music
- Trays and other accessories that can corral everything you need to hold you in place. I have a "resting tray" in my living room and another near my bathtub.
- Incense and beautiful incense holders
- Absorbent materials, to keep sound and light from bouncing around the space
- Layered bed linens in multiple levels of softness and tactility
- A color palette with a low intensity; hues can be rich but not bright or highly contrasting, or too wide-ranging.

A STUDY IN PASSIVITY

RETREAT &
RESTART

NICOLE WAS RECOVERING from a traumatic divorce when she enlisted my help. She was using only half of her apartment, which had two bedrooms and two large living spaces, as if occupying only half her life. As she grieved the loss of her marriage, she had thrown herself into work, completely ignoring her home. Her apartment had become a crash pad rather than the healing space she needed.

We began by switching up the rooms, moving her bed into the former guest room, painting the walls a pale blue, and adding a soft, thick rug. This gave her space to restore her energy and begin to go through her healing process, rather than run away from it. We hung family photos and added heirloom furnishings (a chest of drawers, her grandmother's upholstered chair) to trigger warm memories and remind her of less painful times. We transformed the bedroom she had shared with her ex-husband into a yoga and fitness room and infused active energy into it with plants and a bold wallpaper to motivate her toward her fitness goals. We then set up a living area near the kitchen, across from the window with the nicest view. Now she greets each morning in this sunny, high-energy spot. We added a live-edge wood table (nature symbolizes new growth) and two chairs to offset loneliness by encouraging her to invite friends over. A gorgeous chandelier hangs overhead. Crystal and other glass pieces throughout the apartment fill the space with reflected light. Many passive elements we brought in—soft colors, cozy textiles, and familiar, comforting objects—allow for retreat and rehabilitation. In the end, Nicole gained license not only to fully occupy her home but also to reclaim it as a space of nourishment and self-care.

Passivity &
the Bedroom

Passive energy is gentle, positive, and compassionate, yet our culture has us wired for a nonstop crash-and-burn cycle. Growing up, many of us were taught to prioritize hard work above everything else, and we have internalized that message. As adults, we feel tired constantly. We are not trained to recognize what adequate rest does for our mind or body. Yet we need downtime more than we care to admit.

So, how do we design bedrooms for optimal rest? First, recognize them as spaces for deep slumber, where you can release all exertion. The function of a bedroom is to eliminate movement, so add furnishings that encourage extended lounging. Having a minimal bedside setup is soothing, but if you must get up repeatedly, it's not allowing for true rest. Be proactive instead, and trick it out with everything you need to stay put.

The quality of evening light in a bedroom is key. By that I mean not only what comes from the bulb but also from the materials of the fixtures themselves, especially the shades. If you have standard white shades, for example, consider replacing them with custom shades in colors and textures that foster passivity. The amount of light cast makes a massive difference when you are in your night routine—and in the morning, too. Make your transition from sleeping to the early-morning hours more intentional with tiny lamps and candles. Both are soft on the body, as they don't create an excess of light to jar you awake.

If you have chairs in your bedroom, pair them with ottomans, as elevating feet not only improves blood flow but also settles an overextended nervous system.

The goal is to up the softness factor throughout the bedroom, and nowhere is that more crucial than in the textiles you choose. Layer in textures that feel good on the skin, in the bed linens but also on other tactile surfaces. Ask your body what it likes touching most and program that response accordingly, so that the feel of fabrics and other materials on the body is soothing and settling. You want to be able to lean into your headboard and feel supported, so avoid slatted or metal headboards that don't allow the body full respite.

Finally, expand the relaxation experience in the bedroom by way of sensual details, using natural light, aromatherapy, soothing sounds, soft things to touch, and rituals like warm tea in late afternoon or early evening. By reinforcing the energy of passivity at every turn, you are generating momentum for more softness in your life, more access to body wisdom. You are telling yourself, "I recognize the need for more gentleness in order to access deeper body wisdom."

Reducing the color contrast in a bedroom eases an overly stressed nervous system. The narrower the palette and the more textiles you weave throughout the space (rather than layering them only on the bed), the more soothing the room will feel.

QUESTIONS FOR THE BEDROOM

To foster passivity in the home, start by defining creature comforts for yourself. Think of how you treat a loved one who has just returned home after a long day and is feeling depleted. "Don't get up," you say. "I'll get it for you." Care for yourself the same way and consider the following:

- How do I wind down and recharge?
- What do I need to keep me from getting up again once I lie down? Does my nightstand hold things in place?
- What makes my body feel cared for?
- What energy do I want to feel when I first wake up?

FOUNDATIONAL FURNISHINGS

- An upholstered headboard for maximum comfort and softness
- Soft cozy rugs so your feet have a soft landing when you get up
- A chair with an ottoman (if space allows), as putting your feet up activates "rest and digest" mode
- Closed-door storage rather than shelves to house your functional items and cut down on visual noise
- A nightstand with drawers rather than doors to minimize the need to get out of bed

VISUAL CONSIDERATIONS

- Furniture and accessories marked by harmony and balance. Nothing too jarring or arresting.

- Soft, subdued colors: pastels, anything earthy, rich, or neutral (though dark colors can evoke wombs, programmed deep in your subconscious mind)

- Lamps on dimmers and candles in various sizes and styles

- Light, airy curtains near areas where you can nap and lounge during the day

OPTIONAL ADDITIONS

- Upholstered window seats and nooks

- Soft textured throws and blankets

- Soothing art on the wall across from a resting spot. Maybe an enlarged photo of a favorite landscape; you can put a shelf underneath or nearby to hold a few small but meaningful objects.

- Soft drapes, relaxed Roman shades, or blackout shades to give your body the experience of darkness for a full body reset

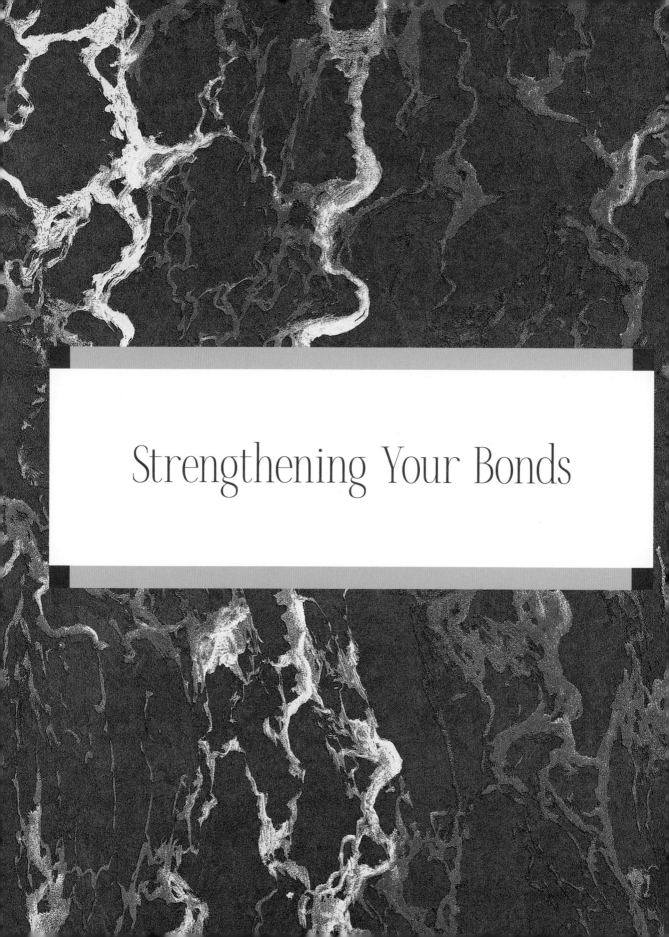

Strengthening Your Bonds

Connection

Whether you're an introvert or an extrovert—or, like most of us, fall somewhere in between—connecting to others is vital. And connection comes in many forms: Maybe you're looking for a romantic partnership. Or perhaps you're already partnered but your relationship could use some reinforcement. You may have children at home but no place to bond as a family. Or you're simply looking to socialize with your friends more often or strengthen your ties with neighbors.

To foster any kind of connection, notice how the roadblocks that are holding you back are mirrored in your home. Sometimes they are obvious: Your living room furniture pieces don't visually connect with one another. It's hard to keep the conversation going between humans when the whole space feels disjointed. Other clues are more subtle: You may say you want people to hang with you in your open kitchen, but the stools you've placed at the island are backless and hard. You're not even aware of the unwelcoming energy those stools have brought into the space, but you end up cooking alone, and hosting dinner parties loses its appeal.

When you make relationship building a primary intention, you can begin to design for embodied connection. The key comes in knowing how to create visual harmony between furnishings. Objects that share similarities carry on silent visual conversations with one another, creating specific invisible shapes throughout the room. For example, the red linen of a chair may speak to the red square in a piece of art and the red bowl on your bookshelf (for more on this, see page 252).

When you want to entertain more guests in your home, consider how you want them to experience a warm welcome. This involves some projection on your part. Think through what is comfortable and inviting and then work that into the design even when guests are not there; that same energy will play out later. You are planting the seed for your future guests, lavishly, with attention and foresight. Create space in the closet for more coats, place a side table by every armchair in the gathering spaces, and put guest towels in the bathroom. Turn off overhead recessed lights and create a more inviting atmosphere with a combination of table lamps and floor lamps. Light lots of candles to make being in the space a more sensual experience. Stock an abundance of napkins, glasses—all the stuff you need for entertaining. When this becomes second nature to you, then having more connection in your life will, too. Think of it this way: If you build it, they will come.

KEY WORDS

Warmth
Companionship
Harmony

Conversation
Bonding
Consideration

KEY FURNISHINGS

- Sectional seating
- A side table or coffee table in easy reach of all chairs
- Storage pieces that accommodate the needs of many
- Furniture (chairs, bedside tables, lamps) in pairs and multiples, to program companionship
- Plenty of armchairs and occasional chairs that can be pulled together for large gatherings
- Game tables in living rooms and other hangout spaces

Fig. 1

Fig. 2

Fig. 3

Fig. 4

Fig. 1 *Round tables eliminate any "head of the table" dynamics.* **Fig. 2** *To encourage conversation, try tucking the television into a large shelving unit, which keeps it from being the center of attention.* **Fig. 3** *Generously proportioned coffee tables in family rooms double as surfaces for game playing and takeout-and-a-movie nights.* **Fig. 4** *Make sure that any artwork in your bedroom symbolizes the intimacy you want in your life. This painting of Krishna and the Gopis, from the Hindu tradition, strengthens the intentions of mutual devotion and partnership.*

Use matching rugs in different areas of a large open space to reinforce the energy of connection. To strengthen that integration, repeat the colors on opposite sides of a room once more, to keep the walls in dialogue.

KEY DETAILS

- Chairs facing a sofa, as if they are in conversation
- Framed views with strong focal points (to draw people in)
- Flower-filled vases and pots, colorful signs of welcome
- Floor pillows and loungers as extra seating
- Photographs and family heirlooms that reinforce a sense of togetherness
- Baskets with lids to store toys and games and to hold extra throws and blankets
- Vintage items to provide a sense of warmth, especially in modern homes
- An art gallery wall around the TV in the living room (having something interesting to look at when the TV is off encourages other kinds of togetherness)
- Artwork in the bedroom that encourages union (i.e., no solitary figures)

A STUDY IN CONNECTION

CREATING CLOSENESS

TOGETHERNESS AND INTIMACY don't always come naturally at home; oftentimes you have to tip the scales to call those feelings forward. When Alysa moved into the Dubai home she shares with her new husband and his two teenage daughters, for example, she found the surroundings cold and distant. Rigid, even. Long before she arrived, the house had been arranged primarily for function and order, with sleek, angular furnishings and hard-edged surfaces. There was nowhere to sink in and settle. In order to encourage a closer, more tight-knit family dynamic, she was looking to warm up the space and create an atmosphere where the family could form new bonds and strengthen existing ones. She envisioned time spent together over daily meals and on larger occasions while gathering with their extended family.

In a few months of solely online meetings, we hatched a plan to shift the dynamics of her blended family's home through intentional design choices. Alysa then executed the plan, starting with the kitchen. She added a table for four, so everyone in the family could share meals every day. Because the existing dining room was small and without good light, it wasn't used often. So, we moved the fourteen-seat dining table into the oversized foyer, where the twenty-foot ceilings gave it more room to breathe. Next, we suspended a series of beautiful pendant lamps to bring the eye up. Now when the extended family visits, they enter a magical space designed for togetherness at the table. It feels more inviting and accommodating right from the start. The former dining room was divided into a few different zones, with comfy chairs for watching movies, playing games, and reading. Any formerly unused (or "dead") spaces are now reimagined.

The house's functionality remains intact, but the mood is much livelier and homier. We were able to create much-needed spaces for connection in the kitchen and dining areas, as well as in the living area with a large sectional, a crucial marker of stability. We gave that piece its own makeover, too, replacing the brown leather with a durable light linen and streamlining the number of cushions to create a less cluttered look. At the same time, we injected a nice jolt of stability with soft floor coverings that feel good underfoot and fluidity (the multi-use space has seating for groups of all sizes, including all the relatives) without having to completely overhaul the home.

Connection &
the Living Room

Living rooms don't often fulfill the promise of the name. The truth is, even if spaces are beautifully appointed, unless the warmth of togetherness is woven into their fabric, the effect on the body is the opposite of living. As a result, the space lies dormant and people-free, sadly.

How, then, do you encourage actual living in communal spaces, which also include family rooms, dens, kitchen and dining areas, and outdoor gathering spots? Start by digging into your vision of what the room can be. List everything you want to occur there, and all of the people who will use it, including future guests and visitors. You will quickly realize that it takes some rethinking to achieve the potential of the space.

Our emotional intelligence grows when we are able to plug everyone's needs into these gathering areas, continually refining those needs as they shift. When you weave such harmony into your home, your body receives several messages: You can welcome people in and still be comfortable as you make space to engage with them, listen, and communicate freely. Guests intuit that they can relax and experience the pleasure of interaction.

Experiment with different layouts of your existing furniture: Put yourself in the shoes of everyone you hope will enter your space, and let your body tell you what arrangement feels best. Consider the pieces as if each is a person and you're orchestrating their placement to encourage more connection. If all your seating is facing one way, for example, you are not encouraging conversation. Arrange pieces to face one another instead, to increase engagement.

If you have a large open floor plan, look to the living spaces of traditional manor houses, which are divided into smaller, more intimate seating arrangements. Composing "rooms within rooms" allows multiple activities to happen at once without competing for space and attention. For example, a little nook with a daybed creates a resting area for someone who wants to share space but not conversation. Put a small round table in a sunny corner of a living room for eating and drinking or engaging in hobbies like puzzles or games.

Focus on walls, ceilings, and floors to strengthen connection. Consider installing wallpaper or painting the walls a color to help the space feel cozier. Paint the ceiling or treat it in some other visually arresting way. Avoid empty corners, which look neglected and lonely. You want to feel embraced from all corners of a room.

At-the-table dinner parties were on hold for the first few years of parenthood, so my partner and I turned a long dining table in our loft into a console to create more floor space for the kids to play.

QUESTIONS FOR THE LIVING ROOM

Consider how your home can promote meaningful, embodied connection at every turn, the same way that someone planning any social event might. Think of how people will physically interact with one another in the spirit of comfort and ease—close but not overly crowded, together but not packed in tight. Consider the following questions:

- Do people regularly connect with one another in my home? If not, what's holding them back?

- Are larger pieces arranged in the most cohesive way? If not, what alternate arrangements can I try?

- Can I set up more than one "room" within the room, to facilitate multiple activities at once, and spaces to be "alone together"?

- What kinds of memories would I like to create in this room?

- Where do people sit? Are they too close or too far apart?

FOUNDATIONAL FURNISHINGS

- Various seating options. Aim for as many as the room can comfortably handle. Position the largest upholstered piece first, in the spot in the living room with the best view outdoors (aka the money spot).

- A fluffy rug large enough to hold the key pieces of furniture—and the whole room—together

- Varied lighting options for varied scenarios: large groups of guests, a small dinner party, just your family, you alone

- A bench at the foot of the primary bed to visually unite the two sides

- A console behind the sofa as an extra surface for hors d'oeuvres and drinks when entertaining

VISUAL CONSIDERATIONS

- Furnishings and accessories that are visually integrated and balanced on each side of the room

- Diverse materials in the space rather than one element used over and over again

- Filled corners; in large rooms, avoid emptiness in at least two of the four corners (try round tables, daybeds set beneath large indoor trees, folding screens, and items on pedestals).

- Images within the space that promote connection. Try to mix family photographs in with other meaningful images rather than fill a whole wall with portraits (hallways are fine for those).

OPTIONAL ADDITIONS

- Poufs for extra seating
- A large coffee table that doubles as an impromptu dining surface
- One long horizontal decorative pillow on the primary bed to signal connection
- A large woven textile above the bed, so that there is nothing heavy hanging over your heads
- A well-styled coffee station in the kitchen, with beautiful trays and accessories, to encourage lingering on weekend mornings

Back-to-back sofas separated by a large console table create two seating areas in my large-scale living room, making more space for multiple conversations at once. I purposely kept the area between one of the sofas and the daybed open, for ease of movement. There is intentionally no overhead lighting, only lamps, so evening scenes are more subdued and intimate.

Sculptural Chairs

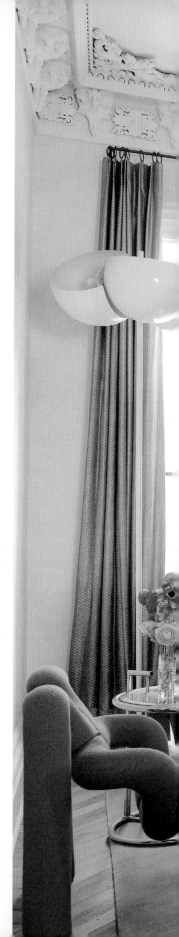

ALL CHAIRS ARE NOT CREATED EQUAL. Some are designed for sinking into and settling in, and others, like office chairs, for sitting upright and at attention. Sculptural chairs, on the other hand, serve beauty more than function by standing out and making a room more visually appealing. You are meant to admire them. These furnishings are marked by bold shapes or colors (and in some cases, both), and they never fail to shift the balance of a space.

Adding a sculptural chair is a low-effort way to inject seriously eye-catching presence and punctuation into a room. If you are in a place in your life where you are hesitating (such as when you are dreaming of turning your side hustle into a career), use one as the physical embodiment of decisive action.

Sculptural chairs can be left empty or used as platforms to hold a pile of books, decorative objects, or even a stack of towels in a guest room. They may get pulled in as extra seating at a cocktail party—just don't expect anyone to sit there for too long!

For statement pieces like sculptural chairs, choose shapes that are decidedly different from the profile of your largest upholstered item. Here, the soft, wavy curves of the chairs are juxtaposed with the boxiness of the tufted sofa.

Making Space for Solitude

Privacy

Whereas passivity is designed to regenerate and re-center the body, privacy lets you tune in to your spirit. Designing a home with privacy in mind means deliberately making room for solitude, which allows your body to connect to intuition and engage in a dialogue with the self.

In our daily lives, we distract ourselves in any number of ways. Whether or not we are aware of it, we regularly turn our attention outward and drown out the inner voice. It's become the norm to consume media when we are "relaxing," making no allowance for silence—visual, auditory, or otherwise. Through silence, we connect with our innate wisdom and strengthen our ability to perceive. Think of how many people have aha moments in the shower, the one place of privacy many of us inhabit daily.

As you make room for privacy within the home, consider the distinction between loneliness and solitude. The former is a negative emotional experience. You can feel lonely even in a crowded room. It's what we intentionally avoid when we design for connection. Solitude, by contrast, is a choice we make to actively engage with the self, to be contemplative and open. In solitude lies pleasure. And wholeness. Private spaces let the psyche know that you can be alone without being lonely, that solitude is sacred. They train your mind to perceive a wider view. Through somatic intelligence, you begin to sense your body co-regulating with the space around you.

No matter the size of your home, designate personal space for everyone who lives within it. Practically speaking, that may mean an entire room for meditating or another daily pursuit, or areas within larger rooms—even a piece of furniture that's off-limits to everyone else, where the user can reclaim their attention from the smartphone, the schedule, the flood of distractions and jumbled thoughts. Consider establishing a dedicated corner, fashioning a private space in an alcove, or even reconfiguring a closet. Tuning in to Future Self energy for just a few minutes every morning provides invaluable guidance.

There are no set design rules about private spaces; material choices are best tailored to personal preferences. Beyond that, consider arrangements and furnishings that establish boundaries and delineate personal zones. The more we tap into our own distinct experience of privacy, the more adept we become at interacting with others. That's because this energy also teaches you to hold space and respect boundaries.

KEY WORDS

Intuition
Self-worth
Silence

Contemplation
Guidance
Meditation

KEY FURNISHINGS

- Love seats, especially on large landings or under stairs, to serve as reading nooks
- Folding screens, open bookshelves, and other room-dividing strategies that allow people to claim their privacy in public spaces.
- Storage ottomans to hold supplies for personal pursuits (like yarn and knitting needles, paint sets, and sheet music)

Fig. 1

Fig. 2

Fig. 3

Fig. 4

Fig. 1 *Beyond bedrooms, unused spaces throughout the home can be turned into private napping nooks with cushions and a curtain.* **Fig. 2** *When work creeps into personal spaces, decorative lidded boxes can be used to mark boundaries. Make it a ritual to put the office away for the night within them.* **Fig. 3** *A wall-to-wall ledge just beneath windows creates more personal space in a home with limited table surfaces.* **Fig. 4** *A table in a rarely used guest room provides the perfect spot for painting or writing.*

One of my favorite design solutions for a lack of privacy, especially in large open spaces, is to break a room into distinct sections with open bookshelves, fabric panels, or airy metal or wood room dividers. Each of these options allows individual areas of these spaces to be claimed for personal use.

KEY DETAILS

- A dedicated table lamp connected to the private area only, so you can turn off overheads and have your own source of light
- Sound-absorbing wall coverings (fabric wall hangings work well for this; see page 250)
- A lidded basket for each person in common spaces so that contents (especially phone chargers) are kept to their owners and are off limits to others; in a shared children's bedroom, color-coded bins and baskets to grant each child a sense of ownership
- Occasional tables assigned to contain the needs of just one person
- Small wall shelves to display the fruits of one's hobby (such as watercolor paintings or embroidered fabrics)

ROOM TO CREATE

ONE OF THE DILEMMAS OF APARTMENT LIVING is a distinct lack of privacy; often, you need to carve out space for everyone who lives within the same walls. Catherine, a radio producer, wanted a room of her own (cue Virginia Woolf) to help her fulfill her longtime dream of writing a novel. She had just moved into a new apartment in Brooklyn with her husband and son and was eyeing a bedroom corner as a potential writing space. (When possible, it is best not to use bedrooms as office spaces because the point of a bedroom is to be passive and to rest.) When I walked through the home, I noticed an even better possibility: a windowless pass-through area that was not being put to use. To reimagine it for her, we chose a bold, warm teal paint that looks good on Catherine, so she could "wear the wall." The deep color was the energy spark that helped her feel motivated, yet the depth of the tone made her feel cocooned. I rearranged a set of vertical bookshelves to run horizontally, so the cramped space appears more open, which helped widen her imagination. Along with a small desk, I installed a comfortable nook for reading and recharging and decorated it with exotic fabrics from her travels, for inspiration.

The reconfigured small space is private, yet still manages to feel expansive and functional, filled with multiple active elements (bold colors, patterned fabrics, the small but sturdy desk) and other furnishings tailored to her need for solitude. Several years later, she credits the space as being one of the pillars that led to a massive growth spurt in her career and well beyond it.

Privacy &
Personal Spaces

Personal spaces are born of the fundamental need to connect with our inner wisdom. We all desire a place to cordon ourselves off from others, disengage, and find room to express our creativity, if only for ourselves. That's the point of private spaces.

In fact, one of our earliest instincts is to claim space of our own. Kids as young as two or three start building forts out of sofa cushions, pillows, and blankets. Within a few years, they're marking their own territory, scribbling "Keep Out" signs and taping them to their bedroom doors.

These areas exist on a spectrum from "alone together" areas that become fully yours when everyone else is out of the house to dedicated rooms for meditation, contemplation, and activity that is not necessarily deadline- or income-driven. There's no pressure to achieve anything dictated by anyone else's agenda in a personal space.

I advise people to lean in to purposeful alone time when they feel that they've lost their inner GPS, as a way to reorient and get back on a clearer path. Begin by identifying a space that can be made up solely of the things that make you *you*. Maybe it's a whole room, or part of a larger one. Anywhere you can give yourself over to your own creativity and reclaim your attention by channeling it, engaging with it, and directing it away from distraction. The body wants to access its own inner nature, even for just ten minutes a day.

Personal spaces can be designed for different purposes, whether that's teaching yourself how to sit with solitude in meditation, writing in a journal, or engaging in any head-clearing pastime. Wherever you can give yourself time and space to scratch the itch of self-expression. Rooms in which to play a musical instrument, engage in craft or art projects, or learn a new dance move all fill the bill.

If you live with others, devise a plan with everyone's personal interests in mind. If personal physical space isn't available for every member of the household, is there a time when everyone else is out of the house and a corner of the living room can become your own private spot? Or, without a dedicated room of your own, can you convert a large closet into a place to draw or paint, perhaps?

If you live alone, you have license to create personal space wherever you want. Just remember to define it as such, with intention and a clear plan to use it regularly.

To encourage myself to enter an intuitive inner space, I created a contemplation spot in our guest room by swapping a nightstand for a skirted table altar, with space below for storing candles, journals, and incense.

QUESTIONS FOR PERSONAL SPACES

As you set up a space to tap into your inner wisdom on a daily basis, consider the following questions:

- Do I have space in my home that is all my own? Do others honor that?

- Does everyone who lives with me have the same?

- How can I make the experience of being alone more meaningful?

- What tones and textures make my body really drop in? (For me, it is grounding earthy tones of autumn colors. For others, it's shades of white and raw woods.)

- What symbols and images move something primal inside me or open my heart?

- What do I need to engage with silence?

FOUNDATIONAL FURNISHINGS

- Seating that keeps you alert. You want an upright chair or floor seating that allows the spine to be straight.

- Storage within arm's reach. Keep these spaces focused and as uncluttered as possible. Having your journals, pens, art supplies, and such tucked away allows your mind more clarity before you begin to engage in your chosen pursuit.

- An altar (see page 58) in your private zone to encourage the level of inner connection you desire

VISUAL CONSIDERATIONS

- Personal colors and textures (whatever makes each person feel good in their dedicated space)
- Adjustable window treatments, especially in small spaces, that allow you to go inward
- Personal workout spaces don't have to look like your local gym. Employ unexpected colors and art on the walls that tap directly into your inner resolve and motivation.
- Use books in a writing, drawing, or music den not only as resource materials but as a wall to eliminate the distraction of visual noise. To lighten the energy of your creative space, remove the jackets and stack them to form "walls" by color.

OPTIONAL ADDITIONS

- Small speakers
- Plants or other elements of nature, such as flowers
- Scented candles, incense, or another form of aromatherapy (to drop you out of your head and into your senses)
- Individual designated trays in shared bathrooms
- A large glass cylinder full of bath salts by a tub, to encourage deeper detoxes and locked-door lingering
- A mirrored wall (or ceiling) in a small closet-turned–writer's studio, to create a sense of personal expansion

Balancing the Energies in Your Home

When you observe the six energies, you can sense how they directly relate to what feels in balance in your life and what feels out of balance. What is the easiest way to correct any discordance? You are aiming for harmony among all the energies.

For example, if you want more passivity in your life, turn up the volume of this energy in your home. You can decrease active energy by taking away some of the brighter elements. Begin in one room or make smaller moves in different areas of your home. Do this gradually, over the course of days or weeks, until you begin to feel the compound effect of your actions on your mood and life. An experimental and playful approach works best.

As an example of how to use the six energies to meet your emotional needs, I'll take you through how I created more emotional support in the living room (pictured on pages 224–225) of my family's rental space while our "forever home" was being built. As the original estimate of two years' construction time turned into four, I had to make strategic upgrades so that we could experience more harmony without using up our resources—anything that I bought would have to double as an investment for the new home.

Balancing Fluidity with Stability

To counter the feeling that our lives were too in flux, I knew I had to bring in some elements of stability. The many disparate side tables not only felt random but also added lots of little legs to the room. In their stead, copper side tables were chosen for their sturdy legless shape and were positioned to symmetrically flank the sofa. Stone, a quintessentially stable material, was introduced through the X-based marble side table and a heavy travertine table that was repurposed as a headboard for the floaty daybed, providing a solid surface for us to lean against.

Balancing Activity with Passivity

The constant activity in my life at the time created serious burnout, yet there was nowhere in my living room to retreat and get cozy. I wasn't giving myself the opportunity to truly relax in the space. My first act was to release the shapely-but-rock-hard rattan chair on the right (even that fuzzy throw didn't make me want to sit there), and replace it with a super-plush chair and ottoman. This became our emotional regulation chair (see page 25). The result? Fewer child tantrums and adult meltdowns occurred; instead, a new family custom was born. Whenever anyone felt the need to calm down, the chair became our solace in physical form. My son ran to it every day after school to ease the transition to home.

Balancing Privacy with Connection

With the kids getting older, I noticed a family dynamic I wanted to nip in the bud: each of us retreating too much into our separate corners with our devices. The privacy spaces I had created in the room were working too well, and I wanted to make sure we were experiencing the vital energy of connection. Changing out the worn cowhides for our new sisal rugs invited us to get down on our knees and play on the floor together. The purple patterned ottoman in the middle of the room hinges open and is full of games and toys, which expands the options for how we connect. Positioning the sofa toward the large window rather than the TV invited in more face-to-face time.

When I moved into this rental home, I resolved not to buy anything new. Yet the furniture floated around the large open space without a sense of cohesion (mirroring the pattern in our lives at the time).

To correct the imbalance, I brought in a few strategic pieces to harmonize the floor plan. The substantial jute rug holds all the main pieces of furniture, suggesting wholeness and unity. I also re-covered the neutral daybed with a more dynamic patterned fabric that incorporated the colors of the other upholstered pieces, making it instantly more integrated.

PART FIVE

PRIORITIZING PLEASURE

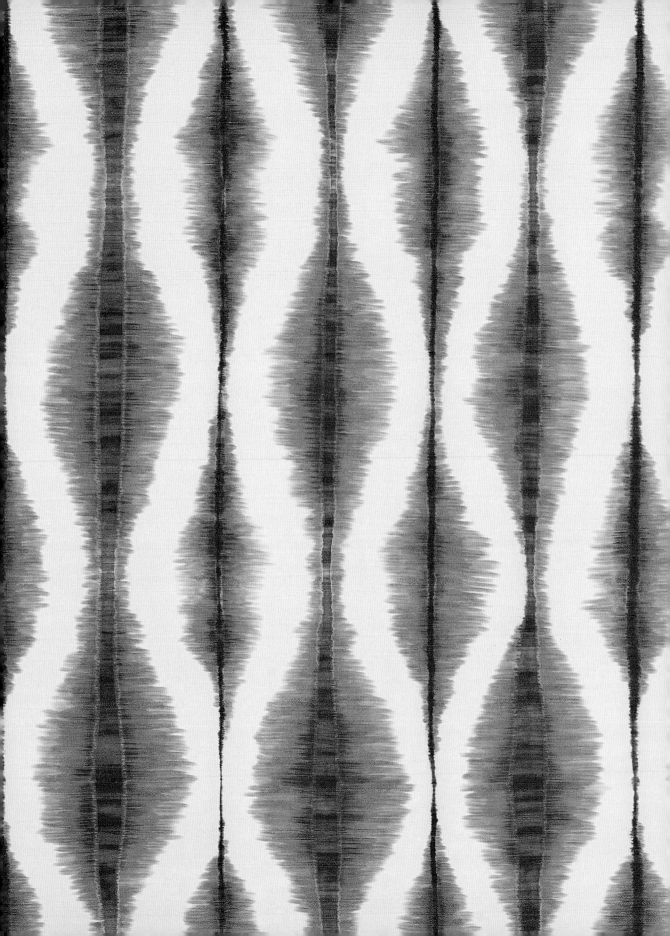

Bring more beauty into your home, and your body will feel the immediate effect.

Once you understand how making small adjustments in your home affects your sense of self-worth and helps regulate your emotions, your home begins to arouse more pleasure in your body. There's no denying it. This is what I mean when I say (as I often do) that you can use your home to turn yourself on. Your intention in accessing the power of the physical realm is to be lit up, so that the act of moving through your home becomes more pleasurable. And pleasure is inherently magnetic. When your physical surroundings align with the intentions you expressed for your lit-up-by-life Future Self, you magnetize the essence of the future into the present moment.

Up to this point we've largely focused on looking inward, closing your eyes and seeing yourself and your home—past, present, and future—with the mind's eye. We learned how to code your home deliberately, starting small and working your way up to bigger, more immediately impactful moves. Here, we will focus on the physical realm, which consists of everything that you can detect through your senses—sight, smell, hearing, taste, and touch—and its relationship with your body. Through the lens of your body, your home is a self-programmed sensory experience.

Understanding how beauty works is key, primarily knowing how it can be employed as a tool, for both pleasure and purpose. Beauty generates heightened energy, and heightened energy feeds you.

When you imbue beauty with meaning, you tap into the potential of the physical world, surrounding yourself with elements that strike chords deep within and learning to code your home for more fulfillment, more meaning, more joy.

In the physical realm, we take what you learned about looking inward and bring it forward, into the external world, and then back again. This is the full-circle feedback loop of Spatial Alchemy.

Here, we examine the life-changing effect of being seduced by your home, of viewing it as a partner. You will use the elements of the physical world to step into your desires, stoke them, and magnetize them in a way that maintains a pull on your body and brain. The more you cultivate that pull, the more alive you feel. This creates the relationship of oneness within the home and beyond. The compound effect of living in a home that lights up your senses is nothing short of magical.

On the following pages, you will learn:

- How to use beauty as a tool to capture and focus your attention

- How to purposefully experience more delight in your home and yourself

- How to translate the energy of the Future Self into the physical space of your home—its four walls, roof, and floor, and all the stuff contained within

- How to mix the elements of design—color, shape, texture, and the like—with awareness

- How to create cohesion between furnishings and other objects

- How to release yourself from aspirational notions of taste and generate authentic self-expression

Let's Get Physical

Most of us never learned to have an active dialogue with our own body's intelligence. Instead, we were taught to prioritize our logical minds, and we ended up with our thoughts racing in a constant loop. Growing up, I was steeped in the traditional Western, talk-centered approach to mental health. I did talk therapy regularly from the time I was a teenager until well into adulthood. The treatment was profoundly impactful, but at a certain point, I was talked out. I had reaped as many benefits from this mental approach as I could, but because I was not engaging my body, I was not addressing any of the intelligence that was stored there. And so I sought out experts in the field of somatics.

Somatics is loosely defined as any practice that explores the mind-body connection (*soma* is Latin for "body"). Its focus is on unleashing the inherent wisdom that lives in your body.

Lynn Kreaden, a somatic practitioner, posits that at the same time that you are mentally aware of what you are doing, you can also go deeper, to bring awareness to every part of your body—your feet on the ground, your breath, the softness in your eyes. This goes beyond mindfulness to incorporate embodiment, or the sense of being in conscious relationship with the other realms (spiritual, mental, and emotional) by way of the physical. Embodiment is a key component of somatic intelligence.

Once I set out on the somatic pathway, I experienced a paradigm shift in emotional intelligence, bringing me into an intimate dialogue with my body. The deeper I dove into somatics, the more I realized that working with all of the senses in tandem was like taking the express train to pleasure. As I learned to access this whole-body wisdom—the deep intelligence found in my skin, my heart, my gut—it was as if I had activated my Spidey senses. I could decipher my own cues (even the subtlest ones), which helped me see how to program my home to support my emotional needs (as we covered in Part Four).

Somatic therapist Luis Mojica works with clients to alleviate stress by focusing on the body. A hallmark of this process is creating safe, soothing spaces within their homes that reassure them that all is okay. Understanding how to design a home where you feel safe is, in fact, an important life skill. When I moved from my city apartment to a country house with my family, I felt emotionally uneven. I craved stability and connection, so I used somatic principles to welcome those energies into my home. I started by looking around my bedroom to see how it might provide for me. My nightstand looked cool, but it lacked drawers, so things quickly piled up on top of it. This left me looking at a mess right before bed every night and the minute I woke up in the morning. A sense of disorganization stayed with me all day. Wanting to change that, I started giving my body the experience of order it needed. I thought through my needs step-by-step, first by swapping out the old nightstand for one with drawers, and then by putting socks in them, so I wouldn't have to go searching for them whenever I wanted to feel cozy. The new nightstand addressed many issues for me. By housing everything in one place, it helped me eliminate the sense of chaos, cleared my sight lines, and gave me a more pleasurable experience each morning. My nightstand, myself.

"My nightstand, myself" is one among many examples of how somatics have informed my home design. I believe every member of the family needs a tactile chair they can call their own, as another example (see page 25 for more). Tactility is a key element of stress alleviation. Think of children who stroke a soft stuffed animal to soothe their emotions when they're upset. When we have trouble bringing ourselves to center, we can use throws, blankets, and pillows to work in much the same way. Upholstery is another factor. Your body can sense the difference between leather and velvet or soft linen, for example, which is more soothing to most nervous systems.

By incorporating somatic practices into home design, you can program your home to give you everything you need to pamper yourself. In the process, you learn to work out any emotional kinks, access the body's natural wisdom, and build capacity to handle change. It's not only about pampering yourself, however. Designing your environment from a somatic perspective also involves training yourself to prioritize body awareness. When your home is attuned to your system, you can meet uncomfortable feelings, sit with them, and ground yourself. This is a powerful tool not only for healing, but also for bringing centeredness into the daily experience of life.

This large open room in our new home is designed to actively engage the senses in order for the whole family to move out of our heads and into our bodies at the end of a long day. I brought in elements that are foundational to somatic therapy practices to help bring us into the present moment. These include one area devoted to sound, with a guitar and record player, as well as other markers of relaxation: soft fabrics, lots of pillows, and books.

TAP INTO THE WISDOM OF THE BODY

Learning to translate your design inspirations into your space involves under-standing design elements—how they work, how to layer them well, and how to use them as building blocks for pleasure. Yet developing a style that resonates with us can be overwhelming. One way to alleviate that pressure is to tap into your body's inherent wisdom by way of the senses.

Start by taking a walk through your home. Following the steps below, scan the space, room by room, and focus on how your senses (apart from taste, which isn't relevant here) respond. You want to gauge where your body experiences expansion, constriction, or numbness. Take your time and tune in to reactions both strong and subtle. Everything you experience through the process is worth noting as you deepen the connection between home and body.

– Sound. Focus on what you hear. Are there noisy areas in your home? Where is it most silent? Do you notice a slight high-pitched hum coming from the elec-tronics? For example, the sound of a dishwasher may be aggravating, while the birdsong outside your window elicits a different bodily response. Similarly, some people find peace and quiet soothing, while for others, a pronounced stillness may be discomfiting. See where you fall within that range as you move through each room and passageway.

– Touch. Slowly move through the home touching a variety of things—the fabric of a chair, the smoothness or roughness of wood surfaces, the cool bumpiness of a wall. Describe the textures you experience. Do specific textures bring up memories? When you see yourself at ease, for example, do you imagine that you're settling into a bouclé chair? Drying off with a Turkish towel?

– Smell. As you enter each space, close your eyes and let your body tune in to this sensory awareness. Where does your home smell good? Describe those aromas. Are there musty odors or overly scented spots? Or pleasantly fragrant areas where you want to linger?

– Sight. Slow down and observe each room, as if you are seeing it for the first time. Try to observe it through only your eyes, not your mind. Soften your gaze by relaxing the area behind your eyeballs and the root of your tongue. What items bring pleasure at the sight of them? What are their colors, shapes, mate-rials? How do the visual relationships between different pieces make you feel?

Do the colors talk to your body? Are they bright and energizing or neutral and calming? How do the shapes of things relate to one another? What's the percentage of rectilinear forms, for example, as opposed to rounded objects?

– Awareness/intuition. This is also known as the sixth sense. Stand in the center of each room and close your eyes. Allow yourself to tune in to the room. How does your body feel within it? At ease or anxious? Begin to feel if the body is expanding in response, or contracting. Does your body feel safe right now?

Now review your responses. The most negative ones will help you prioritize changes. Begin by shifting the most unpleasant things, like replacing trash cans without lids (smell), adding floor coverings to areas without padding (sound), layering sumptuous blankets and pillows onto all-leather seating (touch), bringing in a sideboard for storage when you need to clear a messy dining table (sight), and so on. Use the most positive responses to identify the surfaces and furnishings you want to move toward in other areas of your home. Amplifying your pleasure through the senses, whether adjusting the position of your speakers to direct the flow of sound around a room or infusing a space with incense to encourage your relaxation response, is worth any effort it takes. Be gentle with yourself as you go through the list, however, to avoid getting overwhelmed.

*In this room, I wanted to encourage basking in the warm sunlight, which awakens our inner feline.
I placed a cozy daybed beneath the windows and positioned large-scale plants nearby to evoke
the experience of looking up at trees overhead.*

Connecting to Light

Of all the things I learned to do when I designed stage sets for the theater, working with light may have been the most impactful—and easiest—way to shake up the energy of a scene. Throughout my course of study, I came to understand how light affects mood and experience within any space, and that interiors need different lighting schemes for different times of the day. Think of how you want to light up your home (or not) from morning until evening. What is your lighting setup when you walk in the door after work? While eating dinner and after dinner? When you're lying in bed before going to sleep?

Take the seasons and the activities that will occur in each room into consideration as well. Winter afternoon light has a quality quite distinct from that of summer mornings, for example. Note how the sun moves around your home throughout the day, where the light hits when you're making your coffee every morning, at lunchtime, and just after dinner.

Access to light is essential for optimizing health and wellness. Because the energy of natural light feeds your body vitamin D through your skin, sunlight is the primary design consideration in a living room. Try arranging the chairs and sofa to maximize your exposure to it. Bedrooms are a different story. More often, you want to diffuse the light to create softer, more passive moodscapes.

Consider the following as you enhance the dialogue between the rooms in your home and the sun:

- Enhance sunlight on mantels and side tables or sideboards with colored glass objects like pitchers and vases.

- Add reflective surfaces in sunny spots to mirror and amplify the light.

- Notice the shadows that lamps and other shapely objects cast around a room at different times of day. Try putting specific objects in this path, and watch the shadows move as the sun moves. This is a primary way to relax at twilight.

Fixtures with Impact

If you're choosing light fixtures for function only, you are missing an opportunity. Take recessed lighting, as an example. It's efficient, but if it's the only source of light in a room, the effect can be more corporate than cozy. Instead, rely on recessed lighting to supplement more aesthetic choices, like a vintage chandelier that doesn't cast enough light. Below, a few more light fixture suggestions.

Floor Lamps

Treat floor lamps as the design decisions they are. They can double as functional sculpture; unusual shapes make compelling statements. Consider not only the light they cast but also what their appearance adds to a room visually, and vary the heights of each.

Pendants

Hanging fixtures can be used with abandon, for beauty more than function. Gorgeous chandeliers and sconces work the same way, for visual effect over practicality, which is acceptable as long as you support them with other light sources.

Tiny Lamps

Place tiny lamps on kitchen counters and islands, bathroom surfaces (away from water, for safety), and shelving units. When the main lights are out, their less intense glow gives a sexy, lounge-like vibe.

Custom Lampshades

If your lamps have standard white shades, replacing them with custom lampshades is the best bang-for-your-buck way to create something bespoke. Beyond the improvement in the looks department, pleated fabric, slubby linen, and wood shades cast a soft, warm glow, perfect for downregulating one's nervous system for sleep.

Candelabras

CANDELABRAS EMBODY HIGHLY PLEASURABLE, out-of-the-ordinary moments. The especially warm and enchanting glow they cast feels like gratitude in action. Having a weekly practice of celebrating yourself, your family, and your life sets a festive tone, as if your cup is overflowing. I light a candelabra every Friday night, to announce the end of the week and a transition into the weekend (though I have also been known to light one just to amp up daily life). Like using special-occasion dinnerware every day, actions like this have an instantly uplifting, mood-enhancing effect.

You can also use candelabras for takeout-and-a-movie date nights at home after the kids have gone to bed or on rainy afternoons or winter evenings. Candlelight relaxes the body more than lamplight does.

I like to mix things up, using a chipped painted carved-wood candelabra to add patina to a modern space, for example. In a more traditional home, a simple, streamlined candelabra keeps the vibe from tipping toward "Dracula's castle." Floor candelabras can go very church-like very fast; choose one only if you're design confident. If you're wary, see how a small candelabra feels before working your way up to a larger model.

Forget any preconceived notions of what candelabras look like, and where they have to live in your home in order to cast a magical glow. This clay vine candelabra is a representation of growth and fertility, and reinforces that energy among other decorative elements in this shelf-top tableau.

This Is Your Body on Beauty

From an early age, many of us are taught to believe that beauty is only skin-deep, not worthy of serious attention. But real-world experience teaches us otherwise. Try as we might to ignore it, our bodies are programmed to respond to beauty. There is a magnetizing force to beauty—beyond definition or even language. Your body knows the innate *yes* when it feels it. Something in you expands in response to the stimulus of beauty, drawing you toward an external force.

I've always been fascinated by the relationship between beauty and self and wondered whether the experience of beauty could be quantified. Semir Zeki, a professor of neuroaesthetics at University College London, emphatically believes that it can. With the help of neuroimaging technology, he has discovered that the area of the brain called the medial orbital frontal cortex always "lights up" in response to the perception of beauty, whether visual, musical, mathematical, or even moral. Although each type of experience activates different combinations of areas in the brain, the overlap always occurs in the medial orbital frontal cortex.

Why is this important, and how does it relate to your home?

Consider this: Beauty plus purpose equals power. When you are captivated by what you behold, you can begin to beauty-hack your own brain, using the items in your home to mold pleasure for specific purposes. Add a shake of meaning and association to that beauty, and the possibilities get a lot more interesting —and plentiful.

The more you embed beauty in your surroundings, the more immediate gratification you receive. Rather than chasing or wanting or feeling that you are lacking, you are living inside of *already having*. Beauty is the bridge between these states of being. Every change in perspective, every upgrade within your home, is an opportunity to deliver pleasure to the senses. You are crafting your subjective experience of home.

We've all been in homes that have an intrinsic pull on us, no matter the style. We feel the depth of connection between the home and its owner. They are wielding beauty purposefully, simultaneously addressing the attraction and motivation, aesthetics, and energetics.

Beauty generates heightened energy, and heightened energy feeds the soul. When you form the physical world around you to beautifully reflect your desires for a more abundant life experience, you can deftly weave together beauty and your intrinsic values.

Here is where the energy of the physical realm goes beyond interesting and becomes a call to action: What is beautiful to you, and how can you use that pull for your own benefit?

Note which images and sculptural forms in your home move you, and then experiment with their placement to elicit a greater yes *response every time your body draws near.*

WHAT LIGHTS
YOU UP?

Attraction is an inexplicable bodily response (and not only to other humans). Have you ever felt an immediate physical reaction to a space? A soaring Gothic cathedral, maybe, or a hilltop with a spectacular view? What happens to your body? If you catch your breath or feel momentarily unsteady, take note of that reaction. You can use it later as a compass when designing your home.

Now think back to a time you walked into a stunning restaurant, hotel, or home. Remember your body's response? What specific elements within the space caused your jaw to drop? In the present moment, are there colors, textures, shapes, and lines that regularly produce positive bodily sensations (or negative ones)? Your answers will help determine the mix of materials that your body is drawn to. Keep in mind that a positive charge is not always a jolt. Sometimes a beautifully textured surface makes you want to settle in, or the light in a corner inspires you to curl up with a blanket and a book, or a color encourages you to tune in to the silence rather than engage with an electronic device. Consider the following questions:

– What colors, patterns, surfaces, and textures are you regularly drawn to?

– Which elements that you liked in the past do you still favor? Which have fallen away as you evolved? The consistent ones are key features to take note of as you hone your design voice.

– What design elements remind you of your travels? Are there places you've visited that resonated with you physically? Some people respond to the way that cultures other than their own express beauty. Record that for yourself. I love the lushness of Moroccan design, for example.

– What eras do you find beautiful? Some people love the playful shapes of the 1960s, whereas others are more attracted to the chunky shapes of turn-of-the-twentieth-century Arts and Crafts furniture. Getting to know your go-to eras will help you sift through the myriad options to develop your own coherent design language.

Gallery walls are the ultimate vehicle for self-expression. Keeping the color palette in check helps unify an eclectic grouping of imagery, including paintings, graphic posters, photographs, and three-dimensional items like wall sculptures.

Materializing Pleasure Through Styling

Styling is temporary. That's what I love about it. I can restyle whatever I want whenever I want, to shift energy without breaking the bank. Allowing your body into the styling conversation deepens it.

As you think about styling within your own home, again ask yourself the benchmark question: *What do I want to experience*? We all desire a home that looks good. But more than that, we want our home to *feel* good all over. If you design to invite a specific feeling into your life, you are taking deliberate action steps toward it. Choose the ingredients that create this experience and combine them strategically. This is the gift of styling. Noticing and following the feelings of pleasure will help you in making the larger decorating decisions, because styling is a microcosm of the overall interior design of your space.

Styling may seem intimidating, but it doesn't have to be. The best stylists create coherence among individual pieces. That's it. When an interior is cohesive and balanced, it feels harmonious, no matter how many styles are woven into it. The goal is for it to become greater than the sum of its parts.

Bodies respond to coherent spaces, because they relax the nervous system. Take a moment to imagine the difference between walking into a chaotic home and entering a sacred space. One most likely elicits a subtle recoil in your body, while the other causes your body to open. As a stylist for twenty-five years, I've had the privilege of working with the world's best interior designers in the most incredible homes. My body has received the visceral imprinting of what it feels like to stand inside coherence, over and over. As a way to understand the power of styling, take my dining room, pictured opposite. I have six tablecloths that I cycle through every couple of months, and I use them to inspire quick and easy energy shifts depending on the season and what I sense my family needs in our communal space. I never spend more than an hour restyling, and I limit myself to things I already own, plundered from various parts of the house. Try a similar exercise in your own home, taking an hour to restyle one surface and noting how the change affects you.

Fig. 1   Fig. 2

Fig. 1 *A subtly striped linen tablecloth brings a gentle, passive but playful energy to the dining room. I paired it with a transparent resin sculpture in front of the window, to symbolize clarity, and a solid travertine lamp with a metal shade to ground the space.* **Fig. 2** *Same room, different vibe. A boldly colored and patterned textile dials up the fiery, active energy. Once I added a pair of bright red lamps and hung a bigger piece of art on the wall, the room went kapow! Wood elements keep things in balance, as do the round rattan tray and earthy ceramic pitcher.*

This living room offers a
master class in integrating
disparate styling elements to
create cohesion: A collection
of wooden walking sticks on
one side of the sofa balances
the wood of the armoire
on the other. Lamp bases
with seemingly nothing in
common are harmonized
with matte-black shades.
The red frame on a neutral
piece of art ties it in to
the red elements in two
bolder paintings and in
the striking block-printed
pattern on the armchair.

Fabric Wall Hangings

WHEN A SQUARE OR BOXY ROOM calls out for softness and movement, textiles are one super-simple, accessible fix. Think beyond upholstered furniture, pillows, and throws, and consider the possibility of adding fabric wall hangings.

While curtains are helpful, they don't work in all spaces (in modern homes with long rectangular windows, for example, they can look out of place); wall textiles, on the other hand, can fit within a range of decorating styles and spaces. Tapestries and large-scale woven wall hangings do double duty, serving as art and bringing much-needed texture and dimension to walls. They make grand gestures in spare, minimal spaces, without tipping the balance too heavily, the way an abundance of other textiles might. What's more, they help bring the eye up and inject pattern into a room in a low-commitment way.

And unlike other decorative accessories, a fabric wall hanging is easy to make yourself. Find a patterned fabric you love, and sew a channel into one end to fit a curtain rod. Then hang it from the ceiling or on a wall. Alternatively, consider hanging a rug on the wall—a common approach in many cultures—for soundproofing, warmth, and coziness. Doing so in a small room, like a library or guest room, can instantly make it feel more inviting.

Fig. 1

Fig. 2

Fig. 3

Fig. 4

Fig. 1 *Hanging a woven textile above the tub softens the sleekness of a white-tiled modern bathroom, injecting warmth and color.* **Fig. 2** *Large patterned textiles replicate the punch of wallpaper without the messy (and often costly) installation.* **Fig. 3** *A voluminous curtain with an exaggerated tassel tieback adds richness and sensuality to this bathroom, where it functions as a room divider in the absence of a door.* **Fig. 4** *Antique tapestries of bucolic landscapes can be used to suggest an idyllic view from the bedroom.*

When Color Meets Your Body

Color is the language of energy and intuition. Australian painter John Russell called it "energy made visible." Yet color is also a science. Many cultures have used color and light therapy as a core tool in healing, from ancient Chinese medicinal practices to modern-day meditation. This is because color has a profound effect on your body; there is also a direct relationship between color and the chakra system (see page 140). Deep oranges, for example, correspond to the second chakra, specifically as it relates to desire and eroticism; I use orange in my bedroom to support this aspect of my partnership. Purples and indigos on my altar activate my crown chakra (the seventh chakra) and expand intuition (the sixth chakra). Green is the color of the heart chakra (the fourth chakra), so using it in living rooms helps create the experience of embodied connection.

The mood of any room is created by color, but it's an active rather than passive process, defined by your awareness of the *whys* of your choices. Following are some general principles for bringing color into your home.

- Be judicious in your color choices and avoid going to extremes. An all-white or otherwise colorless scheme, for example, can feel demanding and constricting.

Conversely, the more color is in a room, the richer and more vibrant the space can feel—but a home with too many colors can make it impossible for you to think straight or relax.

- Designing a room with similar-toned neutrals and light woods can be calming but also one-note. To prevent neutral rooms from feeling bland, bring in a contrasting base note, like an earthy dark brown. Consider other colors that work with neutrals, like mustard yellow or olive. These "almost neutral" colors create visual interest without standing out too much.

- Triangulation is a powerful technique (think of the Egyptian pyramids). When something is repeated or echoed three times, it carries weight, both physically and energetically. To create cohesion, repeat any color that you bring into a space twice more within it. Imagine each color as its own language; its repetition invites conversation rather than a series of monologues.

- Consider the finishes, too. Whether a surface is matte (light absorbent) or high-gloss lacquer (which reflects light) will influence the way that colors affect you emotionally and physically.

Fig. 1 *Adding a jolt of color, like this cobalt blue shade, is one lightning-fast way to inject energy onto a neutral base.* **Fig. 2** *Burnished colors bring a more nuanced depth to a room than a bolder hue would; here I used a burnt-orange linen to cover the walls of a windowless pass-through room.* **Fig. 3** *Bright yellow and soft green carry from one space to the other here, for visual continuity and a strong "come hither" pull to the bedroom.* **Fig. 4** *Especially vibrant walls need no artwork or other embellishment to make a statement, especially when they're paired with furniture of an equal intensity.*

Fig. 1

Fig. 2

Fig. 3

Fig. 4

If you have a hard time creating a color palette, let a favorite pattern do the work for you. In this living room, the print on the matching armchairs inspired the scheme for everything around it—not only the larger items like the bookcase, rug, and sofa but also smaller ones like books and bowls. Together, the elements create symmetry that extends from the floor to the topmost shelves, created a powerful, pulled-together energy.

When Texture Meets Your Body

How can you use texture to make your home a more pleasurable place to be? Bed linens are one of the easiest items to play around with as you explore texture. The most sensually styled beds feature a variety of fabrics—quilted and woven, silky and smooth, slubby linen and crisp cotton—within a limited color palette, so your body experiences the gamut of textures without getting distracted by other senses.

There are practical considerations to texture as well. Do you want to encourage more order in your life, for example? Or more relaxation? Rooms with predominantly hard, shiny, and smooth textures appear streamlined and sleek, and can represent structure (or encourage it). By contrast, spaces marked by soft, matte, and rough textures are generally more relaxed and rustic. Picture silk pillows and then linen pillows—you get the idea.

The textures of a room exist in relationship with one another. What is the balance between rough and smooth within a particular space? Hard and soft? Shiny and matte? Counteract smooth-textured spaces, like kitchens and bathrooms marked by sleek cabinets and counters, with textured items like woven rugs, slubby fabric shower curtains, and trays with a pronounced wood grain, as a few examples among many.

Think of how the sound of static grates on your nerves. The same irritating effect results from an excess of visual texture—a hodgepodge of pillows, say, or a surplus of materials with multiple finishes. As an antidote, remove highly textured and irregular items first, and then gauge how the room feels. When you're ready, introduce a few smooth and structured pieces, like a shiny tray or a polished stone lamp.

Plants are big texture amplifiers, and adding them is one of the easiest and quickest ways to soften any space. Consider the relationship of plant to pot. A fern in an aged terra-cotta vessel will give you an entirely different experience than one in a shiny metallic cylinder. Aged and patinated items, too, are especially effective at bringing textured depth to modern spaces. The rougher the surface, the more it will offset sleekness. Try incorporating an item or two (max) with a rough, chipped patina; any more than that and the room may start looking shabby. Books also amplify texture, especially when they are gathered together on a bookshelf. If displaying only books (without tchotchkes), loosely group them by color and separate the colors with blocks of white or neutral spines. This will reduce the weightiness of a too-dense wall of books.

An array of similarly textured elements can serve as the foundation for a multilayered space. Here, the woven floor covering, blinds, chairs, and pendant coexist beautifully with an abundance of patterned tiles, textiles, and decorative plates.

Thick-Pile Rugs

To soften any room, even in an austere modern space, try adding a rug with a thick pile. These textural workhorses are a tried-and-true way to enhance embodiment in the home, which helps when you are looking to regulate your emotions with the energy of passivity. Somatic therapists believe in the power of stretching the body on the floor and rolling around or lying flat on the floor to find your grounding and get centered.

Many of us experience the floor only with the bottoms of our feet; a thick-pile rug allows for yummy tactility underfoot. Consider the areas of your home where you are most inclined to lounge and put the thickest-pile rugs there. You'll have more places to stretch out after work or whenever you want to relieve stress, practice breathing exercises, or meditate.

The range of styles for thick-pile rugs is wider than you might think, from Beni Ourain Moroccan rugs to retro shag carpet. If you have thin rugs, you can mimic the effect of a thicker pile by using rug pads. One of my tricks is to layer two rug pads to make a thin rug feel extra cushy. Just be sure the dimensions of the pads are about an inch smaller than the rugs all the way around, to avoid tripping hazards.

In our previous home, I used a thick rug to as an opportunity to sit together with my kids on the floor and occasionally eat dinner at the coffee table.

Spot the pairs of opposites in this room: Fiery red pillows contrast with the utilitarian quality of the plywood walls, while the antique artworks in distressed frames counteract the stark modern lines of the daybed. Curved table legs bring movement to the boxy forms in the space.

Opposites Attract

Ready to disrupt stagnant energy? Juxtaposing stylistic opposites should do the trick. Imagine a bright 1960s plastic lamp on a traditional sideboard, say, or a diminutive side chair upholstered in bold, patterned fabric. These powerful pairings work well in streamlined rooms, immediately upping the interesting factor. Aim for every room to have three juxtapositions to prevent it from looking matchy-matchy.

If your space feels bland, it may be weighted heavily in the direction of one color or material. If so, invite its opposite into the mix. For example, if you have a room that is wood-heavy (floor, baseboards, doorframes, furniture), work against the surfaces of the materials. If the wood is primarily smooth and shiny, introduce some rough and matte surfaces, like a few highly textured tall ceramic vases. Conversely, bring in a smooth metal cylinder lamp with a structural metal lampshade to an interior dominated by rough-hewn, industrial-feeling wood.

Shapes, too, can be juxtaposed to unlock energy. A large, amoeba-shaped tray visually breaks up rectangular countertops like a charm. Curvy lamps look great in front of a gallery wall of rectangular art. If your sofa is boxy, make sure that either your end tables are round or your coffee table has some curve to it (especially if you're looking for more flow in your life).

As you work your way from room to room with the energy of friction in mind, consider the purpose of each space and whatever it is you are hoping to offset as you play with the juxtaposition of opposites. For example, when your bedroom feels too basic—all white cotton bed linens and white walls—soft layers of opposites will add depth without taking it out of the calm zone. First, consider a large vintage-patterned rug in a muted color scheme. The patina of vintage items offsets the crispness of all-white bedding and walls, and the subtle pattern serves as a counterpoint to all the solid color in the room. Take the color you love the most in the rug and buy simple linen curtains for the windows, to contrast with the bedding. Finally, consider what you will see across from your bed, and play with scale—large art in small rooms is its own form of juxtaposition.

This integrated room is another study in harmonizing polar opposites. *Antique and modern forms coexist: The black and white pieces are softened by the warm tones of leather, wood, sheepskin, and animal prints, and the sisal rug and throws balance the smooth coated metal of the coffee table. In a restricted color palette like this, the shape of each piece of furniture is accentuated.*

Bringing the Eye Up

Planes are the structures that create a room—namely, the floor, walls, and ceiling. Look at planes horizontally, dividing the room into thirds in your mind, then study the way that furnishings and decorative items exist within those divisions. This means that furniture legs and low items are in the first plane, seating and tabletops are in the second, and any elements with height—tall plants, pedestals and plinths, artworks, moldings, picture rails, and such—comprise the third.

In contemporary design, the emphasis tends to be on the bottom two thirds. The top third is often overlooked, especially since invisible recessed lighting is ubiquitous. But this shift can lead to a sense of heaviness. Consideration of the top plane is key to a well-balanced design. To infuse a room with more of a sense of fullness, which has a profoundly energetic effect on the body, it's important to draw the perspective all the way up to the ceiling. (Remember, as legendary fashion editor Diana Vreeland said, "the eye has to travel.")

As you design with all three planes in mind, don't ignore the ceiling. This often-overlooked surface offers a nice opportunity for deliberate design, especially in small spaces like foyers or powder rooms. Paint the ceiling a different color from the walls, even if the shift is subtle, or hang wallpaper on its surface, to make a significant statement at small expense. (For renters, stick on/peel off wallpaper is readily available.) I love painting ceilings of pantries, laundry rooms, and other "work" areas in unexpected colors, to bridge the mundane and the beautiful.

In a café-style dining nook, a visible border between walls and ceiling mimics the effect of old-world architecture. Though the bespoke embellishment appears refined, a similar look can be achieved with grosgrain ribbon, a glue gun, and a steady hand.

Arranging artwork to travel all the way up the wall is an excellent example of emphasizing architectural planes in action; in this case, the trick amplifies the spaciousness of the high-ceilinged room. Creating a tableau of "look at me" objects atop a bookshelf lifts the eye as well.

PUTTING PLANES TO USE

As you begin to think about how to use planes strategically
to impact your living spaces, consider the following:

1. Furniture that is too leggy can look confusing and disordered
   in a dining room. One way to avoid this is to choose a dining
   table on a pedestal base or one with slabs of wood holding it up.

2. Consider a ceiling treatment in your bedroom, to channel the
   energy you want more of as you are in your bed looking up.
   A slight variation of (or in harmony with) your wall color can
   be grounding, particularly if the wall paint is dark. The high
   contrast between dark walls and stark white ceilings found in
   many bedrooms often begs to be softened.

3. When there are few walls in an open-plan space, the ceiling lights
   should create cohesion visually, in color, material, or shape.

4. Putting art over doorframes achieves two goals: It marks the
   crossing of a threshold and draws the eye up.

5. Floating shelves are another easy trick-up-your-sleeve way to
   break into the third plane.

6. Arranging pieces in the same color, material, or texture in
   different planes within a room encourages the eye to travel.

SPACE SHIFTERS
Pedestals

I LOVE USING PEDESTALS to reinforce positive patterns: They lift things up, literally, and make bold, dramatic shifts that telegraph confidence to your brain.

I use pedestals to fill empty corners, displaying large vases with big branches or dried floral arrangements or highlighting large sculptural pieces. If a beloved piece feels too puny for the pedestal, I will use a stack of white or neutral books to lift it higher. I prefer thick column pedestals over the skinny-leg variety, to symbolize solidity. Spindly ones often feel like they will tip over if you come too close.

Pedestals also create drama in the middle plane of a room: When you visually divide your room into vertical thirds, most of the action is at the bottom third (rugs, upholstery, tables). There is typically little to see in the top third (hence my love of large art, painted ceilings, and chandeliers) or in the middle. Pedestals serve as great equalizers, balancing the three planes. I especially like a pair of matching pedestals; the symmetry is immediately stabilizing, with a time-honored, regal aesthetic.

A large, boisterous plant atop a sturdy pedestal can be especially dramatic in a crisply tailored room. The jolt of energy is palpable here, thanks as well to the juxtaposition of an antique urn with a lacquered plinth.

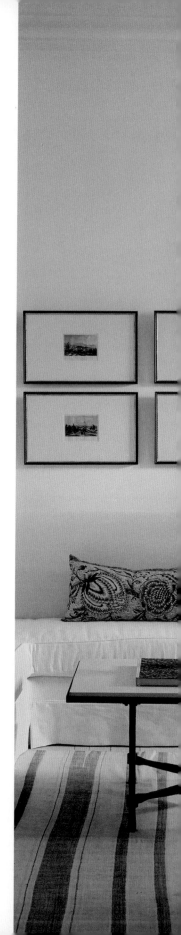

Being Home

So here you are, a Spatial Alchemist. You've released outdated identities, upgraded your routines, learned how to code new mental and emotional patterns into your surroundings, and started to put together a home that lights you up. In doing so, you've seen the surprising interplay between your home, your psyche, and your life. You recognize that your relationship with your home is ever evolving, which runs counter to much of what we are taught to believe about interior design. Instead of striving for the dramatic "before and afters," "gut renovations," or "instant makeovers" you see on reality TV, you're ready to let your home slowly develop along with you over time. If you think back to every home you've ever lived in, you'll see that they have gradually shaped you as much as you've shaped them.

My hope is that as you go forward, you will use this book as a road map, turning to it when you're ready to make a major life change as well as when you just need to choose a new tablecloth. That you'll revisit the exercises in these pages when you're feeling stuck, and they will prompt you to shake things up accordingly.

Above all, remember to take pleasure in the process: Begin small, gain confidence, fine-tune your stuff, then circle around again and adjust as needed. And, likely, adjust again until you note a difference in yourself. Live with this new arrangement, track what happens in your life as a result, gain more confidence, make an uncharacteristic (even uncomfortable!) design choice or two, and then sit with it for a while and see what happens. Ask other members of your household what they need, and adjust. Invite people over and note how it feels to have them in your space. Buy something slightly extravagant and see how that affects you, in an ongoing cycle of reassessing, releasing, and rearranging. Then take a breath and once again do nothing for a while, until you recognize a new desire in your life. Invite it in by planting its seed in your home.

And on and on, and delightfully on.

Further Reading

Below is a list of books that informed the development of Spatial Alchemy.

The Architecture of Happiness by Alain de Botton
"Beauty is the promise of happiness," a quote from this treatise on the psychology and philosophy of architecture, strongly impacted how I view the connection between happiness and physical space.

Atomic Habits: Tiny Changes, Remarkable Results by James Clear
I have read this book at least five times. There is absolutely no better process for creating, embedding, and maintaining habits—and so much of that work begins at home.

The Authentics: A Lush Dive into the Substance of Style by Melanie Acevedo and Dara Caponigro
The wide range of homeowners featured in this book are examples of the power of designing your authentic self into your spaces. I see this as one of my style manifestos, which I frequently turn to for quirky, unusual inspiration.

The Beauty of Everyday Things by Soetsu Yanagi
This ode to quotidian objects illuminates the influence these items have on us as we interact with them each day. A poem of a book.

The Body Keeps the Score: Brain, Mind, and Body in the Healing of Trauma by Bessel van der Kolk, MD
Considered the "somatic bible" by many, this book has taught me the profound wisdom the body holds and the subtle but impactful conversation between the body and the home.

The Book of Symbols: Reflections on Archetypal Images from the Archive for Research in Archetypal Symbolism
This comprehensive illustrated compendium of global symbols is a must-read if you are looking to deepen the dialogue between your subconscious mind and your home.

Breaking the Habit of Being Yourself: How to Lose Your Mind and Create a New One by Dr. Joe Dispenza
All or Dr. Dispenza's books have had a profound positive impact on my thinking and my life. For the skeptics out there, among which I count myself, Dispenza's work bridges science and spirituality. It will also show you how to rewire your brain to make measurable changes in any area of life.

The Creative Act: A Way of Being by Rick Rubin
For those who want to hone their manifestational repertoire, this book will teach you to live in a "creator" state of being. For those who want to dial in to the next chapter of life, you will learn how to become a better receiver of whatever wants to flow through you.

Decorate Like a Decorator: All You Need to Know to Design Like a Pro by Dara Caponigro and Melinda Page
If you love interior design, this expansive tome will help you take your skills to the next level, offering tricks of the trade—from when

to upholster pillows on the bias to how to beautifully curate a collection of plates to hang on a wall.

Frequency: The Power of Personal Vibration by Penney Peirce

Before reading this book, I wasn't even aware that I had a vibration that was unique to me, and that I could dial in to it to more intentionally affect my life circumstances. The result was a more conscious relationship with my perceptions.

Homes for Our Time: Contemporary Houses Around the World by the editors of Taschen

The homes in this book series span the world and delight me. Design lovers, prepare to be inspired by colors, textures, incredible architecture, and a wide range of design voices.

The Intention Experiment: Using Your Thoughts to Change Your Life and the World by Lynne McTaggart

For this 2007 book, author, public speaker, and health magazine director Lynne McTaggart created experiments with renowned scientists to test the astounding effect intention has on results. When you see the data from those experiments, your mind will be blown, as mine was. The power of intention is real, not woo-woo.

The Kemetic Tree of Life: Ancient Egyptian Metaphysics & Cosmology for Higher Consciousness by Muata Ashby

This book about the Ancient Egyptian tree of life provided me with a map for how to take the etheric (i.e., the Future Self) into the material world. These concepts form the DNA of the mysticism of the West. Approach this volume as you would a college textbook; it is not a light read.

Man and His Symbols by Carl G. Jung

Jung was one of the most influential alchemists in psychotherapy and is my personal hero.

This book is a classic that delves deep into the interplay between symbols and the unconscious mind.

Mindful Living: A Guide to the Everyday Magic of Feng Shui by Anjie Cho and Laura Morris

A beautiful exploration of the dialogue between energy, your home, and your life, linking Eastern ideas with Western definitions and expression. The power of finding the palettes that resonate best with us is especially meaningful to those for whom color is a language.

Paths of Wisdom: Cabala in the Golden Dawn Tradition by John Michael Greer

Published in 2017, this book provides a deeper understanding of the esoteric transitions of the West that had been systemically eradicated from the mainstream. It showed me the very practical magic of wielding "inner" alchemy to bring about surprising outcomes in the outside world. It also explains the relationships between the mental, emotional, physical, and spiritual worlds in an ecstatically mind-opening way.

The Secret Teachings of All Ages: An Encyclopedic Outline of Masonic, Hermetic, Qabbalistic & Rosicrucian Symbolical Philosophy by Manly P. Hall

This thorough history of the world's esoteric traditions spans psychology, mythology, religion, and philosophy. It is indispensable in understanding how the mechanisms of embodied creation work and how they were used by our ancestors and alchemists throughout the ages to achieve specific results. For history buffs only.

Simple Shui for Every Day: 365 Ways to Feng Shui Your Life by Amanda Gibby Peters

This book showed me the causal relationship between one's home and one's life through a modern feng shui lens. The premise—that feng shui doesn't have to be complicated—delighted me. It is a 365-day-a-year actionable guide, with easy practices that move the needle in your life in surprising ways.

Acknowledgments

To those who pulled this book out of the ether and into form with me:

We met at the beginning of our careers, Lia Ronnen, and working with you over the years, in different collaborations, has been a true blessing. You saw *Spatial Alchemy* as a book before I even became aware of that possibility. Thank you for opening this beautiful portal I get to walk through.

Ellen Morrissey, where do I begin? I am so grateful to you for creating an actual book out of my wide-ranging and sometimes very abstract ideas. How can I thank you enough for your innate understanding of the meaning of Spatial Alchemy? Your incredible patience with the stretches and turns of time that it took to get this thing to the printer was so graceful. You are my midwife, and I could never have created this book without you. We birthed this together.

Bridget Monroe Itkin, thank you for knowing how to translate these methods and ideas into an easy-to-understand system. You are the stability to my fluidity, and I admire your wordsmithing, your organization, and your patience (especially with me). And I couldn't be more appreciative of the time and the love you put into this project. So grateful for you, mama!

Giulia Garbin, thank you for your gorgeous eye, your calm energy, and your incredible talent, which brought this book to a place I could not have imagined possible. I've loved every moment of our collaboration, on every facet of *Spatial Alchemy*. Your design DNA is woven into these pages.

Abby Knudsen, your organization, resilience, and get-the-job-done poise meant so much to me. I loved working with you. Thank you so much.

And a big thank-you is also owed to the rest of the incredible, übercreative Artisan team: Laura Cherkas, Sibylle Kazeroid, Suet Chong, Nina Simoneaux, Annie O'Donnell, Nancy Murray, Zach Greenwald, and Rebecca Stepler; the magical, portal-creating publicity and marketing team of Ilana Gold, Abigail Sokolsky, and Theresa Collier; and David Schiller, for seeing *Spatial Alchemy* and for your openness to my work.

Kitty Cowles, thank you so much for your supportive and solid guidance during the book proposal phase, your discussion of strategy, your (multiple) explanations of contracts, and your tough love as you coached me across the finish line. You have my back, and knowing that has been vital during this book creation process.

▲▲▲

To my dearest friends and career collaborators who were indispensable both to this book and to my life:

Thank you for being my friend, mentor, sister, and way-shower, Elizabeth Mayhew. Whenever I am at a career crossroads, you show up to point me in the right direction. I don't know where I'd be without your support of me and my work. I love you so much.

Dara Caponigro, it is hard to express the depth of my gratitude for your influence in my life. Thank you for opening so many doors for me, both career-wise, as a mentor, and as a sister who has walked the path with grace. You live in my heart.

Thank you so much for the gift of your photography for this book, Melanie Acevedo. I feel honored to have your pulse beating within these pages. I have always admired you not only for your amazing talent but also for your humor, your depth, and your generous heart.

You and your magical quintessence have expanded me on the level of soul, Gillian Pothier. I am honored and blessed to have you in my life as a friend and collaborator. You have infused your depth, your gnosis, and your precise language into *Spatial Alchemy*. I will always be grateful to you for the electricity and magnetism that knowing you has brought into my world (both personally and professionally). You inspire me to no end.

Inessa Razumnaya, words can never convey the depth of gratitude I have for your walking into my life. This book could not have been created without you, nor could our home or home life in general. There is a karmic thread between us, and I will adore you forever.

Catherine Burns, your sparkle, intelligence, and friendship touch my heart and soul. Thank you so much for sprinkling your genius on the preface and afterword of this book. Your ability to magic my story into words formed two bookends that expressed the me of me.

My spiritual li'l sister, Michelle Adams, thank you for your love, your loyalty, and your generosity of spirit. You are one of the kindest people I know. Your patience in showing this grouchy Gen Xer how to make Insta reels, and your guidance and support of *Spatial Alchemy*, has me bowing down to you in gratitude. I adore you, always and forever.

Nicki Clendening, I've stood in admiration of your incredible style, your eagle eye, and your beautiful way of putting things together for so many years, and I'm so thrilled we've found our way into a nourishing friendship (and dialogue about our favorite topic: design). Thank you for your counsel on this book, your counsel on my home, and your calming presence while I was on an emotional roller coaster.

Stacie McCormick, I knew we would be friends as soon as I met you. I extend so much gratitude to you, mama extraordinaire, for your discerning eye and heart of gold. Thank you gifting your time and love to this book. You gave me the confidence to keep moving forward when I felt really stuck.

Thank you so much, Frouwje Pagani, for taking me under your wing as soon as you met me. You single-handedly saved my career in the magazine industry by showing me how to be the most amazing assistant I could be. I love the beautiful balance you are able to maintain between your career, your creativity, and your family life.

Trish Lyons, you've been such an incredible professor, mentor, friend, and art collaborator. I am so honored by the work we did for *Dream Wider*. It was a joy playing in the visionary sandbox with you. Someday, this project will happen. One way or another. I love you so big.

Lesley Unruh, a million hugs and tears of gratitude for your beautiful work chronicling my homes through the years. Your warmth, your generosity of time and spirit, and your understanding, creative eye are woven throughout this book, and I'm so grateful.

Thank you so much, Annie Schlechter, for letting me comb through your incredible archives day after day. I feel blessed to have your electric, colorful work (and energy) within these pages.

Damaris Drummond, you are one of the warmest spirits I've ever met, by your very nature. Thank you for your care and love—of our family and of Spatial Alchemy. Blessings on your home.

▲▲▲

To the many experts I interviewed for this book, from many fields—scientific, psychological, and spiritual:

What would my life be without you, Shana Lory? You are a pivotal and primary person in my daily life. Thank you so much for all the wise counsel you gave to me while I was writing this book—on motivation, on self-discipline, and on how to transmute metaphorical lead into gold.

When I first met you, Jamila Reddy, I noticed how present and grounded you were—you have natural wisdom in your bones. Thank you for the never-ending, powerful conversations we've had over the years about the fine art of manifestation, the life skill of balance, and how to use our everyday rituals to bring the pleasure that sparks the manifestation.

We've done it all together, Lynn Kreaden, from women's groups, to somatic work, to healing, to collaborating. I adore you. Thank you so much for your support of me, my work, and this book.

Nerding out on the causal connections between home and life has brought magic to my world, and few people are more fun to trade home magic spells with than you, Amanda Gibby Peters. Thank you for twice taking the time to be interviewed for this book.

You've been such a fixture for me in my somatic journey, Barbara Droubay, helping me access pain in my body and rewire it. I am so honored to have you in my life. Thank you for the term "embodied creation."

Jessica Fern, until I read *Polysecure*, it didn't occur to me to design my home to help heal my disorganized attachment style. This understanding was a pivotal key that your work helped me access. I feel very honored to discuss the interplay between secure attachment practices and one's home with you. Thank you so much for your time.

Thank you, Natalie Cohen, for the wisdom and perspective you shared, as both an elementary school teacher and now a therapist. Understanding the rituals kids learn to feel safe and secure during transitions has been invaluable to the emotional regulation chapters in this book.

Much gratitude to ancestral healer and coach Ashley Johns for speaking with me about how to weave the past and the future together through the honoring of ancestors in the home.

Your scientific expertise was invaluable, Vaughan Gray, in the research and development phase of this book.

I appreciate the gift of your time, Ohad Pele Ezrahi, to hear my take on how different emotional energies relate to the Kabbalah. Feeling secure that the path I was going down had a spiritual foundation gave me the structure I needed to write this book.

I didn't want to stop the conversation when I was interviewing you, Judika Illes, especially when we touched on how to collapse and expand time and other forms of fourth-dimensional magic. Thank you for your care and graciousness.

Jason Nunes, I appreciate your guidance on character defenses and other psychological patterns we experience. Our conversation was crucial in the research and development of this book.

Thank you for the illuminating conversation on symbolism through the eyes of both Jungian psychology and alchemy, Stanton Marlan. Your expertise was deeply appreciated.

Kathryn Morrison, you make stepping through the fire of your fear look easy. I love how your feminine priestess side coexists with your bad-ass business side. Thank you for your Mexico City stewardship, your belief in me, and the magic we created together.

Your counsel was foundational, Michael V. Smith, in helping me lay the groundwork for this book as well as sharpen the processes of Spatial Alchemy.

I deeply appreciate our conversation, Anjie Cho, and your guidance in helping me understand the common threads between the Eastern tradition of feng shui and the Western tradition of alchemy.

Irene R. Seigel, thank you so much for speaking with me about South American shamanistic traditions and their use of power objects. This conversation informed my understanding of the liminal potential of altar spaces.

I appreciate speaking with you, Pamela Grossman, about the links between the home and esoteric practice and ritual. Thank you so much for your time.

Luis Mojica, not only am I an avid listener of your genius podcast, *Holistic Life Navigation*, I also deeply appreciate your taking the time to speak with me about how we begin to feel safe in the body, how to downregulate the nervous system, and how our home can program a much-needed sense of grounding into the system.

Lara Rosenthal, I so appreciate our conversations about Chinese medicine, clearing stagnant energy from the body, and activating systems to function with more ease. Speaking with you was very affirming and fascinating.

Thank you, Lauren Veca, for sharing your midwife knowledge during this book's research and development phase. I loved learning about the process of somatically letting go in order to birth, which mimics the alchemical process of birthing your Future Self. Finding universal threads is one of my delights.

Martha L. Langer, thank you for taking the time to speak with me about the somatics of color, personal palettes, and color vibrancy. Your passion for color deepened my own.

Who else teaches color through the lens of alchemy, Jesse Bransford?! I learned so much from speaking with you about choosing specific colors to activate possibilities. Thank you for not only showing me your magical home but also spending time with me on Zoom to help with my research for *Spatial Alchemy*.

Neil Goldsmith, I loved our conversation about how we program the home and design to spark transformation, as well as how we work with it to integrate profound transformative experiences.

▲▲▲

To those who contributed gorgeous imagery for this book:

Thank you to all the photographers whose incredible work graces these pages (many of whom I've had the honor of collaborating with for years): Melanie Acevedo, Brittany Ambridge, Winona Barton-Ballentine, Earl Carter, Beatriz da Costa, François Dischinger, Kirsten Francis, Heidi's Bridge, Ditte Isager, Stephen Kent Johnson, Kevin Kerr, Max Kim-Bee, Francesco Lagnese, Pernille Loof, Read McKendree, Johnny Miller, Jenna Peffley, Marta Xochilt Perez, Reid Rolls, Annie Schlechter, Eric Traore, and Lesley Unruh.

So much gratitude to the wide range of incredible designers who gave their blessing to use their work, and their homes, in this book: Michelle Adams, Brent and Josh Beekman, Michael Bruno, Dara Caponigro, Billy Cotton, Daun Curry, John Dransfield and Geoffrey Ross, Susan K. Filter, Brock Forsblom, Fawn Galli, Rebecca Gardner, Eliza Gran, Ellen Hamilton, Micky Hurley, Barbara Jakobson, Samantha Knapp, Ryan Lawson, Sarah Lederman, Katie Leede, William Li, Elizabeth Mayhew, Nate McBride and Kari McCabe, Doug Meyer, Wesley Moon, Marshall Neve, Nick Olsen, Jean Pagliuso, Natalie Randall, Ben Reynaert, Tom Scheerer, Joe Serrins, Rachel Sloane, Gen Sohr, Robert Stilin, Marcus Teo, Calvin Tsao and Zack McKown, Tim Whealon, Alexander Wilson, and Josh Young. Thank you from the bottom of my heart, Clarence House, Pierre Frey, and Schumacher for providing me with your gorgeous textiles to use in this book.

▲▲▲

I'd like to acknowledge the blessing of being part of these incredible teams and the impact these people had on me:

The *Domino* '05–'09 crew: Deborah Needleman, Dara Caponigro, Sara Ruffin Costello, Tom Delavan, Michele Outland, Stella Bugbee, Tori Mellott, Eugenia Santiesteban, Monika Eyers, Kate Townsend Simpson, Stephen Orr, Jennifer Rubell, Chassie Post, Michelle Rubel, Amy Peck, Danielle Claro, Chase Booth, Nicolette Owens,

Stacie McCormick, Lesley Unruh, Kim Ficaro, Lindsay Taylor, Kate Bolick, Rebecca Donelly, and Allison Gambrel. Working alongside your brilliance was a golden age for me. We had such a blast together.

The *House Beautiful* '96–'00 crew, and in particular those I worked with most directly: Dara Caponigro, Elizabeth Mayhew, the late Sarah Kaltman Cantor, Peggy Kennedy, the late Lou Gropp, Carolyn Sollis, Frouwkje Pagani, Melissa Cutler, Lisa Walsh, Sara Bliss, Andrzej Janerka, Susan Zevon, Mary-Ellen Weinrib, Debbie Martin, Char Hatch Langos, Christine Pittel, and Jane Margulies. Being a part of this incredible team felt like a dream come true to a young woman who yearned for beautiful design all her life.

▲▲▲

Thank you to the folks at California Closets, Emtek, Kohler, Little Greene, Robern, and TimberTech for your beautiful products in my home.

▲▲▲

To my clients: Thank you for your willingness to step into the magical potential of your homes.

▲▲▲

To family and beloved friends:

Thank you to those who have been my world since I could remember: Irina Aguirre, Lilly Berelovich, Ariel Daunay, Amanda and John Dawson, Elke Dehner, Mika Efros, GiGi Madl, Alla Mashensky, Luba Raynus, David and Kareen Schulhoff, Lea Thau, and Katya Varlamova.

My gratitude to those who more recently have become deeply woven into my heart: Ali

Beckerman, Yeening Chang, Jayne Charneski, Roya Darling, Maria DeSalvo, Lian DesMarais, Stephanie Diamond, Eva Gajzer, Rachael Grochowski, Esty and Shaya Itkin, Jenny Kaplan, Casey Karr, Maria Lomanto, Mitch Martinez, Melanie Meltzer, Sara Mencher, Emily Morrison, Shira Newmark, Isaac Paulman, Ramat, Amy Shapiro, Rachel Shapiro, Zviyah Rachel Smith-Coté, Alexandre Tannous, Hana Cali Williams, Yuli Ziv, and Bliss Zolov.

A special thank-you to the late Faina Anufriev, who was the spark that ignited my inner design fire. Something was born in me when I first entered your home at sixteen years old. It was the first home I'd ever seen in my life that lit me up like a bolt of lightning.

Thank you to my grandmothers, grandfathers, and ancestors for your tenacity and grit.

Thank you to my mother, Lilya Naiman, who taught me to always look within. I really appreciate your being willing to heal our relationship from the roots up alongside me. This deeply contributed to the way I show up in the world.

Thank you to my late father, Daniel Naiman, who taught me the power of self-discipline. Thank you for having the fire energy to get us out of the Soviet Union. I'm forever grateful for the incredible education and support you provided me.

Thank you to my sister, Julia Naiman, who is an embodiment of quintessential "mama energy." I love how you love your kids and mine. And I love you—more than you know.

Thank you to my beloved extended family living in New York, New Jersey, Massachusetts, California, Florida, Israel, Germany, Ukraine, and Russia. My dream is to have my home be a place where we all gather.

Thank you to the Smith-Gusmano clan—Anne, Traci, Robbie, and all your kids and grandkids—for making Mike who he is.

Lucia and Laszlo, I am blessed to be your mother. Thank you for your grace with my often-overwhelmed self while writing this magical book. You are always and forever the gold at the end of my rainbow.

And finally, thank you to my partner in life, my beloved home base, Mike Smith, for putting up with the lesser-evolved aspects of my nature. And for your belief in me and us, despite the choppy waters we navigated together over the last years. You teach me to give and receive unconditional love, the greatest gift of all. Here's to Eden.

Index

Page numbers in *italics*
indicate photographs.

A

abundance
    exercise for, 80–81
    scarcity to, 78–79
activity
    about, 169
    examples of in design, *139*, *171*, *172*
    home office and, *176*, 177–181, *179*
    key details regarding, 173
    key words for, 170
    passivity and, 137, 223
    study in, 174–175
air symbols, 113
alchemy, history of, 14
altars, *50*, 58, *58–59*
animals, as symbols, 112
articulating desires, 20, 21
attachment theory, 28
attraction, exercise for, 244
auspicious chi, 46
awareness, importance of, 25

B

backdrop, home offices and, 178
balance, 22
base, building secure, 28–29
beauty
    exercise for, 244

response to, 243–244
    as tool, 228
Become One with Your Future Self
    exercise, 52–53
bedrooms
    author's, 36, *37*
    passivity and, *190*, 191–193
belief systems
    exercise involving, 84–85
    functioning of, 78
    limiting, 92
    self-worth and, 71
    unpacking, 68
beliefs around wastefulness, 95
big-picture intention, 22
blind spots, 92, 93
Body Choreography exercise, 90
body-sustaining energy, 42
bringing the eye up, 264, *265*, *266*, 267
building secure base, 28–29

C

candelabras, 240, *240–241*
case studies
    activity and, 175
    connection and, 201
    fluidity and, 163
    passivity and, 189
    privacy and, 217
    scaling up, 86–87
    stability and, 148–149
chairs, sculptural, 208, *208–209*
chakra system, 36, 140–141, 252
childhood homes, impact of, 26, 28

Cho, Anjie, 46
clarity, coding for, 126, *127*
clutter, 41, 94–95
coding
    beauty and, 228
    for clarity, 126, *127*
    for dignity, *120*, 121, 122, *123*
    generating momentum with, 121
    for levity, *124*, 125
cognitive dissonance, 61
Cohen, Natalie, 151
color, 48, 252, *253–255*
comfort/style, 82
complaint mode, exiting, 92
connecting to light, *236*, *237–241*
connection
    about, 195
    examples of, *197*, *198*
    key details regarding, 199
    key words for, 196
    living rooms and, *202*, 203–205, *206–207*
    privacy and, 137, 223
    sculptural chairs and, 208, *208–209*
    study in, 200–201
creation, embodied, 54–55
crown chakra, 140–141, 252
cups, as elevating the everyday, *106*, 107

D

daily tasks, 107, 122
decluttering, 94–95
Decode Your Stuff exercise, 99
deliberate design, 62–63, *64*
desires, articulating, 20, 21
details
    for activity, 173
    for connection, 199
    for fluidity, 159
    for passivity, 187
    for privacy, 215
    for stability, 147
dignity, coding for, *120*, 121, 122, *123*
dining rooms, fluidity and, *164*, 165–167
dissolving, 94–95, 99

Droubay, Barbara, 55
duality patterns, 82–83

E

elevating the everyday, 107, 122
embodied creation, 54–55
embodiment, 230
emotional baggage, 25
emotional balance
    exercise for, 138
    introduction to, 134–135
emotional energies, 136–137, *139*
emotional intelligence, 230
emotional needs, meeting, 20, 21
emotional realm, 30
emotional regulation, 134
emotional regulation chair, 25, 223
emptiness, sitting with, 101
energy
    awareness of, 40–41
    balancing, 222–223, *224–225*
    body-sustaining, 42
    emotional, 136–137, *139*
    exercise for, 47
    expansion, 107
    focal points and, *44–45*
    Future Self and, 51
    matter and, 23
    recognizing, 48–49
    soul-sustaining, 42
    tuning in to, 42–43
entryways, stability and, *150*, 151–153
everyday, elevating, 107, 122
exercises
    Become One with Your Future Self, 52–53
    Body Choreography, 90
    Decode Your Stuff, 99
    Identify Your Patterns, 84–85
    Read Your Home's Emotional Balance, 138
    See Your Symbols, 114
    Sense Your Home's Energy, 47
    State Your Intentions for Your Home, 65
    Tap Into the Wisdom of the Body, 234–235
    Three Questions, 32–34

exercises *(continued)*
  Tune In to the Channel, 43
  Use Focal Points with Precision, 117
  Welcome Abundance, 80–81
  What Lights You Up? 244
exiting complaint mode, 92
expansion energy, 107

F

fabric wall hangings, 250, *251*
feelings of safety, 230–231
feng shui, 46, 177
Fern, Jessica, 28
Festinger, Leon, 61
fire symbols, 113
flexibility, 165
floor lamps, 238
fluidity
  about, 155
  dining rooms and, *164*, 165–167
  examples of, *139*, *157*, *158*
  folding screens and, 160, *160–161*
  key details regarding, 159
  key words for, 156
  stability and, 136, 222
  study in, 162–163
focal points, 35, *44–45*, *116*, 117–118, *119*
folding screens, 160, *160–161*
four realms
  diagram of, *31*
  introduction to, 30
framing devices, 49
furnishings
  for activity, 170, *171*, *172*, 178, 180
  for connection, 196, *197*, *198*, 204
  for fluidity, 156, *157*, *158*, 166
  for passivity, 184, *185*, *186*, 192
  for privacy, 212, *213*, *214*, 220
  for stability, 144, *145*, *146*, 152
Future Self
  activity and, 169, 175, 178, 181
  centering, 20, 22, 228
  dissolving and, 94–95
  elevating the everyday and, 107

energy and, 51, 211
exercises involving, 32–33, 52–53, 65
item representing, 104
power objects and, 56
shifts and, 131
symbols and, 109

G

gallery walls, 143, 167, 175, 181, 199, *245*, 261
generating momentum, 121–122
Gibby Peters, Amanda, 46

H

heart chakra, 140–141, 252
holding spaces, 151
home offices, activity and, *176*, 177, 178, *179*
humans, as symbols, 112

I

Identify Your Patterns exercise, 84–85
identities
  outdated, 68–69, *70*, 79, 94–95
  scarcity and, 78–79
inner scarcity, 11
instant gratification, 96, *97*
intention, big-picture, 22
intentional patterning, 26
intentionality, 46, 62–63, *64*, 65, 104–105

K

Kabbalah, 30
Kreaden, Lynn, 230

L

lamps, tiny, 239
lampshades, custom, 239

levity, coding for, *124*, 125
life science, 22–23
light, connecting to, *236*, 237–241
light fixtures, 238–239
living rooms, connection and, *202*, 203–209
love, making room for, 36, *37*

M

manifestation, 54–55
matter, energy and, 23
medial orbital frontal cortex, 243
meditation altars, *50*
meeting emotional needs, 20, 21
mental realm, 30
Mindful Homes (Cho), 46
minimalist/maximalist, 83
mirrors, 74, *75*
Mojica, Luis, 230
momentum, generating, 121–122
Morrison, Kathryn, 71

N

nature, as symbol, 113
negative space, *127*

O

objects
    power, 56, *57*
    with sentimental value, 95
opposites, *260*, 261, *262–263*
outside markers, 51

P

Paracelsus, 14
passivity
    about, 183
    activity and, 137, 223
    bedrooms and, *190*, 191–193

examples of, *185*, *186*
    key details regarding, 187
    key words for, 184
    study in, 188–189
patterning, intentional, 26
patterns
    disrupting old, 20, 21
    duality, 82–83
    emotional, 28–29
    exercise for, 84–85
    identifying common, 82–85
    plant, 113
    seeding new, 20, 21
    self-assessment exercise and, 33
    types of, 129
    unwanted, 25
    use of bold, *128*
pedestals, 268, *268–269*
pendants (light fixtures), 238
personal spaces, privacy and, *218*, 219–221
physical realm, 30, 230–231, 234–235
planes, 264, *265*, *266*, 267
plant patterns, 113
plants, 257
pleasure
    claiming your, 20, 21, 228–229
    materializing through styling, 246, *247–249*
power objects, 56, *57*
power walls, 178
privacy
    about, 211
    connection and, 137, 223
    examples of, *213*, *214*
    key details regarding, 215
    key words for, 212
    personal spaces and, *218*, 219–221
    study in, 216–217
promoting yourself, 72, *73*

R

Read Your Home's Emotional Balance exercise,
    138
recognizing shifts, 130–131
Reddy, Jamila, 54–55, 101

releasing process, 76
re-parenting, 25–26
rooms within rooms, 203, *206–207*
rooms/spaces
    bedrooms, *190*, 191–193
    dining rooms, *164*, 165–167
    entryways, *150*, 151–153
    home offices, *176*, 177–181, *179*
    living rooms, *202*, 203–205, *206–207*,
        208–209
    personal spaces, *218*, 219–221
root chakra, 140–141
rugs, thick-pile, 258, *258–259*
rule bender/rule follower, 83
Russell, John, 252

S

sacral chakra, 140–141, 252
safety, feelings of, 230–231
scarcity
    identities and, 78–79
    inner, 11
scarcity to abundance, 78–79
scenography, 15
sculptural chairs, 208, *208–209*
secular altars, 58
secure attachment, 28–29
See Your Symbols exercise, 114
self-assessment, 32–34, 84–85
self-awareness, 63
self-esteem, 28
self-expression, 60
self-reflection, 22
self-regulation, 29
self-worth, 19, 71, 74, 90, *98*, 122
Sense Your Home's Energy exercise, 47
sentimental value, objects with, 95
shifts, recognizing, 130–131
sitting with emptiness, 101
social comparison, 61
softness, welcoming, *27*, *44–45*
solar plexus chakra, 140–141
solve et coagula (dissolve and coagulate),
        20, 68, 76–77, 94–95, 101, 104, 126

somatics, 230–231, *232–233*, 258
soul-sustaining energy, 42
Spatial Alchemy
    author's background and, 14–15
    feng shui and, 46
    foundations of, 19–36
    Kabbalah and, 30
    process of, 20
    See also individual elements of
spiritual realm, 30
spontaneous/cautious, 82
stability
    about, 143
    entryways and, 151–153
    examples of, *145*, *146*, *150*
    fluidity and, 136, 222
    key details regarding, 147
    key words for, 144
    study in, 148–149
State Your Intentions for Your Home
        exercise, 65
stress alleviation, 230, 231
styling, 246, *247–249*
subconscious mind, 108–109
sun, as symbol, 108–109, *110–111*
supportiveness, 22, *24*, 25–26, 29
symbols
    air symbols, 113
    animals as, 112
    decoding common, 112–113, *115*
    energy and, 49
    exercise involving, 114
    fire symbols, 113
    Future Self and, 109
    humans as, 112
    nature as, 113
    subconscious mind and, 108–109,
        110–111
    sun as, 108–109, *110–111*
    transportation as, 113

T

tactility, 231
talk therapy, 230

Taoism, 46
Tap Into the Wisdom of the Body exercise,
    234–235
taste, transcending, 60–61
tension, 48
texture, *256*, 257
thick-pile rugs, 258, *258–259*
third eye chakra, 140–141
Three Questions exercise, 32–34
thresholds, as framing devices, 49
throat chakra, 140–141
tipping points, 131
transcending taste, 60–61
transmutation, 23
triangulation, 252
tripping hazards, 88–89, 93
Tune In to the Channel exercise, 43

U

upleveling, 14
Use Focal Points with Precision exercise,
    117

V

Vanderbilt, Tom, 61
Vreeland, Diana, 264

W

wall hangings, fabric, 250, *251*
wastefulness, beliefs around, 95
water images, 113
Welcome Abundance exercise, 80–81
welcoming softness, *27*, *44–45*
What Lights You Up? exercise, 244

Y

You May Also Like (Vanderbilt), 61

Z

Zeki, Semir, 243

Photography Credits

Annie Schlechter: 48 (left): design by Brent Ridge and Josh Kilmer-Purcell, cofounders of Beekman 1802; styling by Raina Kattelson; 49 (left): design and styling by Artist Designer Doug Meyer; 112 (right): styling by Annie Schlechter; interior design and *Poultry Suite* rice paper prints by Jean Pagliuso; architecture by Lee H. Skolnick Architecture; 116: homeowners Susan Filter and Peter Koch; 123, 158, 239 (right): design by Houses & Parties; styling by Bebe Howorth; 128: design by Susan Sheehan; 145 (top left): design by Robert Stilin; styling and editing by Doretta Sperduto; 145 (top right): design by Brock Forsblom; 171 (top left), 253 (bottom right): design by Joe Serrins Studio; 176: architecture and interior design by Tsao & McKown Architects; styling by Calvin Tsao; 185 (bottom left): design by Barbara Jakobson; 238 (left): design and styling by Olga Naiman; 251 (bottom left): design by Fran Keenan; architecture by Crystal Tucker with Twin Interiors; 265: design by Micky Hurley; styling by Malu Edwards

Beatriz da Costa: 97, 113 (left): design by Michelle Adams; styling by Olga Naiman; 160–161, 186: design by Dransfield & Ross; 157 (bottom right), 185 (top right): styling by Olga Naiman and Michelle Adams

Brittany Ambridge/OTTO: 185 (top left): design by Daun Curry Design Studio; styling by Martin Bourne

Ditte Isager: 37 (top left), 253 (top right): design and styling by Olga Naiman

Earl Carter: 251 (top right): styling by Olga Naiman

Eric Traore (@erictraore): 75 (top left): design and styling by Olga Naiman

Francesco Lagnese/OTTO: 49 (right): design by Nick Olsen; 70, 91: design by Alexander D. Wilson; 119: design by Tom Scheerer; 251 (top left): design by Benni Frowein (CEO Schumacher EMEA); Roman shade, Maxwell in Mocca by Schumacher; tapestry by Wissa Wassef, Cairo

François Dischinger: 73 (top left), 213 (top right): design and styling by Olga Naiman

Heidi's Bridge: 37 (top right), 124, 139, 202: design and styling by Olga Naiman

Jenna Peffley/OTTO: 240–241: design and styling by Eliza Gran

Johnny Miller: 98: styling by Olga Naiman

Kevin Kerr: 8: design by Olga Naiman; all fabrics and wallpapers from Schumacher; 260: design and styling by Marshall Neve

Kirsten Francis: 100: design and window treatments by Wovn Home; design by Benjamin Reynaert; architecture by Ben Herzog Architect; 146: design by Sarah Lederman Interiors; styling by Frances Bailey; 185 (bottom right), 254–255: design by Rachel Sloane Interiors; styling by Olga Naiman

Lesley Unruh: 2, 13, 16–17, 24, 27, 37 (bottom), 44–45, 50, 64, 73 (bottom), 75 (bottom right), 106, 113 (right), 115, 120, 127, 179, 197 (bottom right), 206–207, 218, 225, 232–233, 236, 247 (right), 258–259: design and styling by Olga Naiman; 35, 171 (top right), 213 (bottom right); 238 (right); 239 (left); 248–249, 270: design by Nicki Clendening; 57, 58–59: design and styling by Olga Naiman; basketball by artist Kehinde Wiley; 157 (top right), 262–263: design by Katie Leede; 213 (bottom left): styling by Olga Naiman

Marta Xochilt Perez: 23: design by Josh Young, Josh Young Design House; styling by Michelle Adams; 157 (bottom left): design by Marcus Teo; 164, 242: design and styling by Natalie and Greg Randall of RT Facts

Max Kim-Bee: 150: design by Dara Caponigro; 197 (top right): design by Timothy Whealon; 197 (bottom left): design by Ellen Hamilton for Hamilton Design Associates

Melanie Acevedo: 48 (right), 253 (bottom left): design by Nick Olsen; 73 (top right), 110–111, 224, 288: design and styling by Olga Naiman; 75 (bottom left): design by Samantha Knapp; 112 (left): design by Windsor Smith for Michael Bruno; 145 (bottom right): design by Elizabeth Mayhew; styling by Carolyn Englefield; 171 (bottom right): architecture and design by Gray Davis of Meyer Davis; 172, 253 (top left): design by homeowner Gen Sohr of Pencil & Paper Co.; styling by Carolyn Englefield; 197 (top left): Rocco Chair covered in Ogden Boucle, Stella Table in Natural Matte, Esmark Sphere Pillow by Schumacher; Gerrits Rug by Patterson Flynn; 208–209: design by Fawn Galli; 214: design by Cliff Fong; 245: design and styling by Ben Reynaert

Patrick Cline for Lonny: 171 (bottom left): design by Nick Olsen; image courtesy of Michelle Adams

Pernille Loof @ Art Department NY: 157 (top left): design by Wesley Moon; 266: design by William Li

Read McKendree/JBSA: 198: architecture by McBride Architects; interior furnishings by Kari McCabe Inc.

Reid Rolls: 75 (top right), 145 (bottom left): design by Nick Olsen

Stephen Kent Johnson/OTTO: 190, 256, 268–269: design by Billy Cotton; styling by Mieke ten Have; 213 (top left): design by Billy Cotton;

251 (bottom right): design by Ryan Lawson; styling by Colin King

Winona Barton-Ballentine: 10, 247 (left): design and styling by Olga Naiman

Images on pages 8, 70, 91, 145 (bottom right), 150, 172, 190, 245, 251, 253 (bottom left), 256, and 260 first appeared in *Frederic* magazine.

Fabric Credits

Clarence House: 32–35: Bodrum in Midnight; 43: Fez Embroidery in Chartreuse; 52–53: Vignelli in Rouge; 64–65, 140–141, 186: Heraklion Damask in Chocolate; 66–67: Cosmico Ikat in Malachite; 90–91: Vernazza in Saffron; 148, 214, 218, 220–221: Borgia Velvet in Peat; 154: Moire Print in Green; 216: Milano Velvet in Claret; 244–245: Traviata in Jonquil

Pierre Frey: 84–85: Ajoupa in Terre; 98–99: Blue Line in Indigo; 114–115: Panthere de Somalie in Somalie; 124: Shiva in Roussillon; 132–133: Florentine in Indigo; 158: Nimes in Cacao; 162: Chaguan in Bois; 164, 166–167: Colombine in Algue; 174: Akbisar in Safran; 182, 234–235: Nimes in Rouge; 194: Portor in Prune; 202, 204–205: Nimes in Corde; 210: Rattan; 213, 236: Shiva in Lin; 218, 220–221: Cymbale in Terre; 226–227: Coban in Cognac

Schumacher: 2: Backgammon Cut Velvet in Green; 6–7, 13: Bellini Silk in Mulberry; 38–39: Sunburst Stripe Embroidery in Black & Neutral; 47: Izapa Hand Woven Brocade in Jewel; 80–81: Zanzibar Linen Print in Cerulean; 86: Tortoise Shell in Amazon; 102–103: Abelino in Camel & Black; 142: Darsy Tree of Life in Sepia; 146: Cordwain Velvet in Olive; 168: Erindale in Americana; 179, 180–181: Franco Linen-Blend Chenille in Indigo; 188: Fondale in Gold; 198: Bellini Silk in Mulberry; 200: Cheetah Velvet in Ebony; 224–225: Piet Performance Linen in Brown; 270: Sabi Tiger Velvet in Java

OLGA NAIMAN has been a New York City–
based magazine editor, freelance stylist, and
interior designer for twenty-five years, and
her work has been featured extensively in
publications such as *House Beautiful*, *Domino*,
the *Washington Post*, and *Real Simple*. Her
unique approach to design, which unites the
spirit, psyche, body, and home for the purpose
of self-realization and transformation, is
called Spatial Alchemy. She currently lives
in the Hudson Valley with her partner, two
children, and pet bunny.

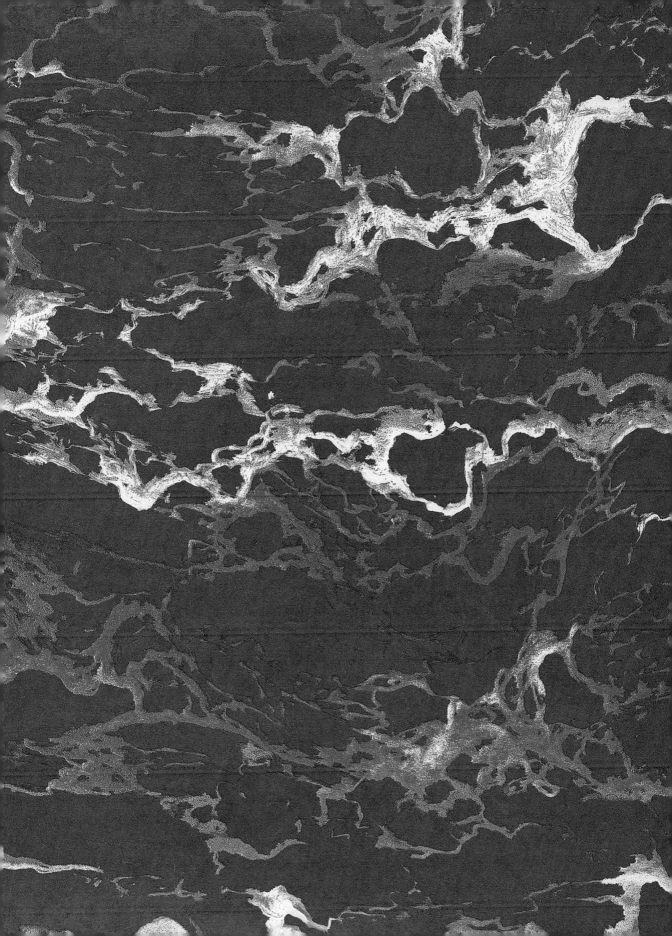

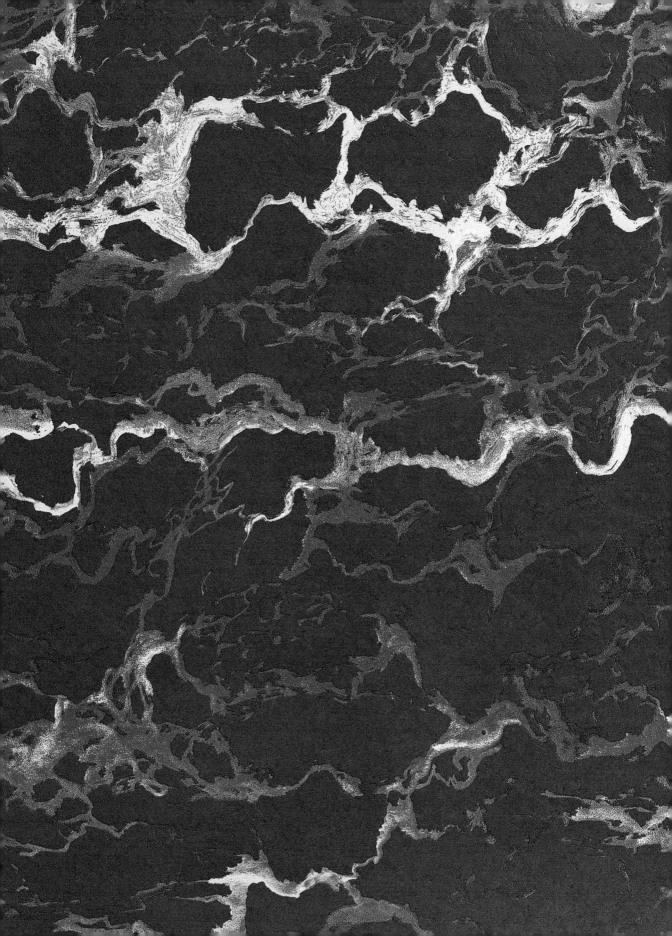